the WINDS of CHANGE

the WINDS *of* CHANGE

HOW ONE ORGANIZATION
TURNED A HURRICANE INTO
A BETTER WORLD

JACK LITTLE

Published by Advantage, Charleston, South Carolina.
Member of Advantage Media Group.

ADVANTAGE is a registered trademark and the Advantage colophon is a trademark of Advantage Media Group, Inc.

Printed in the United States of America.

ISBN: 978-1-59932-652-8
LCCN: 2015959229

Book design by Katie Biondo.
Photos by Rick Rhodes.

This publication is designed to provide accurate and authoritative information in regard to the subject matter covered. It is sold with the understanding that the publisher is not engaged in rendering legal, accounting, or other professional services. If legal advice or other expert assistance is required, the services of a competent professional person should be sought.

Advantage Media Group is proud to be a part of the Tree Neutral® program. Tree Neutral offsets the number of trees consumed in the production and printing of this book by taking proactive steps such as planting trees in direct proportion to the number of trees used to print books. To learn more about Tree Neutral, please visit www.treeneutral.com. To learn more about Advantage's commitment to being a responsible steward of the environment, please visit www.advantagefamily.com/green

Advantage Media Group is a publisher of business, self-improvement, and professional development books and online learning. We help entrepreneurs, business leaders, and professionals share their Stories, Passion, and Knowledge to help others Learn & Grow. Do you have a manuscript or book idea that you would like us to consider for publishing? Please visit advantagefamily.com or call 1.866.775.1696.

This book is dedicated to my family. Their team-like support has encouraged and enabled me to pursue and find fulfillment in serving those who burden my heart.

Thursday, September 21, 1989… Hurricane Hugo blew over Charleston in the very early hours of the morning.

As stated in a 1990 East Cooper Community Outreach (ECCO) brochure: "Just as the winds of Hugo cleared sections of trees and created new vistas, they also swept away the blinders of our complacency that permitted the needs of so many in our area to go unaddressed."

—*Dr. Vic Del Bene*

ABOUT THE AUTHOR

Jack Little has served as the executive director for East Cooper Community Outreach (ECCO) since 2005. He grew up working in his father's business in Columbia, South Carolina, and graduated from the University of South Carolina with a bachelor of science in business administration. He has also earned a master of divinity from Southeastern Seminary in Wake Forest, North Carolina. Currently, he is the pastor of Memorial Baptist Church in Ravenel, where he has served since 2003.

Jack served as director for church and community ministries for the Charleston Baptist Association in Charleston, South Carolina, and the Chattahoochee Baptist Association in Gainesville, Georgia, for more than sixteen years. He founded Charleston Outreach in 1993. He has also served as pastor for churches in North and South Carolina.

Jack has written several publications, including "Making Your Town a Mission Destination," "Training for a World Changer Experience," and "How to Conduct Sports Camps in a Mission Setting." Under his leadership, the Charleston Baptist Association was selected as the National Association of the Year by the North American Mission Board in 1995. In

ECCO received SCORE's National Award for Most Socially Progressive Business in 2009.

1996, Charleston Mayor Joe Riley declared July 20 as Charleston Outreach Day.

In 2014 and 2015, ECCO was selected "Best of the Best" in nonprofits by the *Moultrie News*, and in 2014 the paper selected Jack as the top recipient of votes for the "Ones to Watch." ECCO was honored with the prestigious Angel Award from South Carolina Secretary of State Mark Hammond in 2012. Furthermore, SCORE awarded ECCO the National Outstanding Socially Progressive Business Award and Charleston's annual Coastal Chapter's Non-Profit in 2009. ECCO was also recognized by *Charleston Magazine* and Coastal Community Foundation in 2009 with the Giving Back Award for Community Spirit.

Jack and his wife, Sue, have three children: Watkins, Ali, and Grayson.

Suzanne Flynn, Dr. Vic Del Bene, Liesl Westbrook, and Jack Little at the 2009 Giving Back Awards.

ACKNOWLEDGMENTS

Great accomplishments are made because of many people working together to follow a purposeful vision. First among them are the scores of staff members who have served as foot soldiers—boots on the ground—getting little recognition through the years. Others contributed their knowledge and wisdom, their schooling helping to shape the vision of my ministry. Among these include my supervisor, Mike Williams, who taught me about working with churches in the spirit of unity when I served with the Chattahoochee Baptist Association in Gainesville, Georgia. At the Baptist Association in Charleston, my boss and friend, Dr. Bill Hightower, allowed me to spread my wings and taught me patience in working with staff and others. When I became the executive director at East Cooper Community Outreach, Linda Grausso believed in and helped me better understand the fundamentals of leading a nonprofit organization.

The most important acknowledgement for ECCO's success would be to our board of directors. Through their support, involvement, and guidance, we have grown to serve more people more comprehensively and effectively. Another group to be recognized is our staff. Their commitment and dedication to fulfilling our mission with compassion continues to inspire me and so many others.

Another group of people contributing to the progression of my ministry are the ones who are loyal due to the fact that they really have no choice. I am speaking, of course, of my family.

FOREWORD

The Latin expression *felix culpa* is primarily a reference to the death of Christ on Good Friday, which heralded his resurrection. More generally, the phrase may be applied to any situation that seems terrible at first glance but later transforms into an occasion for growth and positive change.

With that said, Hurricane Hugo was a major *felix culpa*.

On September 21, 1989, Hugo, a Category 4 storm, devastated the Caribbean and then turned its punishment on South Carolina. Its 130-plus mile per hour winds and twenty-plus foot storm surge caused billions of dollars of damage and killed dozens of people. Christ Our King Catholic Church was here through it all and did what we could to help.

Some of the first places we visited were Hamlin and Copahee—small communities on the outskirts of Mount Pleasant, South Carolina. People were living in tents and lean-tos with little food and no electricity or running water.

We soon discovered that this was not entirely the result of Hugo. These impoverished people were at our doorstep before the hurricane. The more we looked around the area, the more we uncovered the truth—the poor had always been there. In the words of Jesus from sacred scripture, Matt. 26:11, "The poor you will always have with you."

However, in our affluent setting, we overlooked them. Something had to be done to help them: hence, the birth of East Cooper Community Outreach (ECCO). East Cooper Community

Outreach began as an ecumenical endeavor, soliciting the assistance of the ministers and pastors in the Mount Pleasant area. United, we would work to fulfill the mandate of Christ to feed the hungry, give drink to the thirsty, welcome the stranger, clothe the naked, and visit the sick and imprisoned.

Over the last twenty-five years, ECCO has grown and expanded in its outreach to address the needs of our community. Jack Little became the executive director of ECCO back in 2005. As an ordained Baptist minister, he has truly made ECCO an ecumenical endeavor. He came to ECCO with vast community experience and contacts.

I express my gratitude to Jack for having contributed so much to the success and development of ECCO as an outreach that is indispensable to the East Cooper area. Jack embodies the spirit of care and concern for the needy for which ECCO was founded.

The miracle of ECCO evolving from one of the worst natural disasters our community has ever seen is best described as *felix culpa*.

Monsignor James Carter
Pastor, Christ Our King Catholic Church
Founder, East Cooper Community Outreach

TABLE OF CONTENTS

A WORD FROM
THE AUTHOR

In this book, my intention is to help the public understand that community-based nonprofit organizations serve the poor and working poor more efficiently and effectively than the government. I also hope to help nonprofits benefit from lessons I have learned, help them create a vision for their preferred future, and show how they can change the direction of their mission.

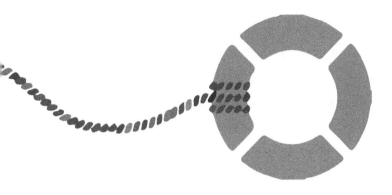

CHAPTER 1
Good from Bad

In his senior year, Irving planned to go to college, but there was not enough money in his family to support his education. A tremendously talented running back for Lincoln Middle High School's football team, he had visions of playing football in college. One of only 120 students in grades six through twelve, Irving was a model student with good grades and impeccable manners, due to the great upbringing by his mom.

Irving was raised in McClellanville, South Carolina, a tiny fishing village (pop. 990) on the Atlantic, halfway between Charleston/Mount Pleasant (thirty miles south) and Georgetown (twenty-five miles north). With few businesses and no industry, career opportunities were extremely limited.

Irving's mother, a single mom, knew he would not flourish if he stayed home. One day, she visited ECCO for emergency food and heard about the organization's Savings Match program from her case manager. The program offers very low-income families a match savings program of $3 for every $1. Money saved over a period of six months to two years up to $1,000 becomes $4,000 with the match. The money can only be used for higher education, starting a business, or buying a first home. To qualify for the match, participants must complete a sixteen-week program, known as Money Smart, which teaches several money management skills, including budgeting, savings, banking, and debt and credit repair.

After hearing about the program, Irving's mother enrolled immediately. She knew this money could help put Irving through college, and she brought Irving in to register for the program the next day. Irving worked at the local restaurant in McClellanville and saved his $1,000 in a six-month period. When Irving's mother reached her total, she put that toward Irving's college education. Through the Savings Match program, Irving was able to have $8,000 to put toward his first-year college expenses.

When Irving made his goal in 2014, our staff had a celebration party for him and presented him his check. He announced he was going to attend Methodist University in Fayetteville, North Carolina, where he earned a halfback position on the football team with a partial scholarship.

This is an example of the opportunity our clients have before them. It's the kind of stuff that bonds our staff together and makes all of our jobs worthwhile. It's what reassures my calling.

Helping people help themselves. What a long way ECCO has come. Ten years ago, ECCO was searching—searching for its identity, searching for its purpose, searching for direction. ECCO was *searching*.

In 1989 ECCO's genesis was in the aftermath of Hurricane Hugo. The storm caused thirty-four fatalities in the Caribbean and twenty-seven in South Carolina. It left nearly a hundred thousand people homeless and resulted in $10 billion in damage, making it the most destructive hurricane ever recorded at that time. The United States and Puerto Rico felt the bulk of Hugo, with $7 billion in total damage in those areas alone.

Charleston County took the brunt of the Category 4 storm, which recorded winds up to 137 mph. Hugo actually landed in McClellanville, which lies in the northern extreme of our service area. Twenty-five years have gone by, and we still hear stories of how the residents took refuge in Lincoln High School, the only school in the community, not knowing the school was just above sea level. The storm surge reached 20.2 feet, and at the peak of the storm, the school began filling with water. It kept rising and rising and rising. Parents stood on top of the tables in the lunchroom, holding their children above the rising tide. No lights. No power.

Today, ECCO is a nonprofit organization that serves a 1,500-square-mile area in the low country of South Carolina. The area it encompasses can be described as northern Charleston and lower Berkeley counties, South Carolina. According to the 2012 US Census data, within our core service area—East Cooper— there are an estimated fifteen thousand individuals who make up the poor and working poor. More than 45 percent of these residents are in rural areas, and 15 percent of residents in neighboring Mount Pleasant are classified as the working poor.

When my service began in 2005, the organization had fallen short of its budget. It was searching for its public identity and making a larger impact in its efforts to serve the poor and working poor. Ten years later, the organization's annual budget has increased 500 percent, from less than $300,000 to just over $1.5 million in 2015.

Our mission has also undergone dramatic change, from giving people fish to teaching them how to fish. Our current mission statement is "to provide safety-net services to low-income neighbors while empowering them to create better lives for themselves, their families, and communities." The public has helped us support this mission through donations of dollars and an increasing number of volunteers.

For me, personally, ECCO has been a very rewarding ministry. The Lord has provided at ECCO as He has at both of the previous ministries where I served. It's very humbling to have the opportunity to share the story of ECCO with you.

TRAGEDY STRIKES

The aftermath of Hurricane Hugo struck a chord with the nation. All eyes were on Charleston, and a national humanitarian effort was launched. Eighteen-wheelers filled with supplies poured in. Disaster response companies and "cowboy" contractors were found in every neighborhood. Homeowners and businesses desperately struggled to bring back a sense of normalcy. Electricity took weeks to return. After a couple of months, the community had the bare necessities to return to basic operation.

Christ Our King Catholic Church, under the leadership of its newly arrived pastor, Monsignor James Carter, responded with emergency assistance of food and clothing to the victims living in East Cooper who remained during the storm. Several local churches were invited to join in the ongoing efforts of serving the needy and poor to supplement government efforts. A temporary relief center was opened on September 27, 1989, and assisted about four hundred families a day to recover from the tragedy.

As efforts continued over the following weeks, Carter and volunteer church members began to survey the area for damage, revealing the deeply rooted pockets of preexisting poverty. The group that would later be named East Cooper Community Outreach (ECCO) realized the greater need to offer ongoing services to those in need. The organization was determined to reach into the community to respond to the needs of the people, evolving from an act of disaster relief into a dependable place for neighbors seeking help. Emphasis was put on providing emergency services to help clients exist from day to day. Food, clothing, and emergency funding for rent and utilities were the sole relief the ministries offered.

The following passages are the personal recollections of Dr. Victor E. Del Bene and Joseph A. Galasso, who in 2014 authored a pamphlet on the history of ECCO in celebrating our twenty-fifth anniversary. In detail, they describe the very first days after the tragedy and the growth of ECCO in the years that followed.

The East Cooper Community sustained extensive damage when Hurricane Hugo hit the area around midnight on Thursday, September 21, 1989. Early the next morning, Father James Carter, pastor of Christ Our King (COK) Parish surveyed the devastation to the church grounds and to surrounding neighborhoods. He was stunned.

Earliest assistance came from COK parishioners. They brought generators to provide electricity for the little chapel. Stella Maris Church on Sullivan's Island had been flooded. The Stella Maris parishioners attended Mass in the COK church on Sunday, September 24. Members of both parishes learned that their school would function as a temporary distribution center.

The center opened on Wednesday, September 27, 1989. Almost immediately the demand for food, clothing, water, and other necessities exceeded available supplies.

A CLOSET, A PHONE, AND A MISSION

Many volunteers showed up to help with the distribution. During those early days, Connie Dopierala and Sister deLourdes Eassy led the effort to untangle the complicated logistical operations. A typical day for them, as well as for others, ran from 7 a.m. to 9:30 p.m. They were nailed often for being out after the 9 p.m. curfew.

At their makeshift headquarters, they had access to one working telephone. It was located in a closet at the Christ Our King parish office. That one telephone and a wall of Post-it Notes allowed them to coordinate the needs of victims with offers of help, to schedule deliveries, and to best utilize the many dedicated volunteers. One kind soul from Atlanta saw the wall of notes and later sent a case of Post-it notes.

An area outside Christ Our King hall had to be set up to handle workers from out of town. This meant tents, cots, and water for showers. Town officials directed the truckers with incoming supplies to the makeshift distribution center. Truckloads of supplies came from nearby and from some distances, such as Michigan, Georgia, Pennsylvania, New Jersey, New York, and Indiana. The Dole Company sent an eighteen-wheeler loaded with pineapple and juice.

Many individuals and groups sent money. One couple called from Michigan offering to adopt a family. Other families offered furniture and appliances.

Mr. Buzzy Newton II of the Piggly Wiggly Company provided food for distribution. It really paid to have Piggly Wiggly's corporate headquarters here in Charleston—Buzzy not only brought the food and all the "fixins," but he also made sure it was hot!

ERGO...ECCO!

When Father Carter and Sister deLourdes checked the damages to outlying areas, they found widespread destruction and debris left by the combination of winds, rain, and floods. They were struck by the startling difference in destruction between impoverished communities and the more affluent communities. They saw that the smaller communities had suffered severe damage, especially to their inadequate housing. This alerted them to the need for a future sustained outreach to those poorer areas.

They had covered the short distance east from Mount Pleasant to the askew Sullivan's Island Bridge, north to Hamlin and Copahee, and as far north as Awendaw.

The devastation to poorer areas presented an opportunity to act on the Gospel mandate to feed the hungry, clothe the naked, give drink to the thirsty, and care for the sick. And that, in turn, would lead to a permanent response to poverty in the East Cooper area.

The original name for the community response effort was Project C.A.R.E. (Cooper Area Relief Effort). Carol Robinson managed the ongoing relief effort. Connie Dopierala, a member of the staff of Christ Our King Parish, acted as coordinator for Project C.A.R.E. Legal advice suggested that the project's name be changed to avoid confusion with the national CARE Project.

The committee had to search for a name that applied to the mission of the movement and its location. Ultimately, Father Carter came up with the winning idea while he was out jogging one morning. The new name would be East Cooper Community Outreach, ECCO.

OVERWHELMING NEEDS

Much like the power of Hugo, the makeshift distribution center at the COK parish was quickly overwhelmed by the flood of needy people and by the volume of food, clothing, and material coming in from the surrounding area and later, from many parts of the United States. They needed more space to help more people.

At the urging of Mayor Dick Jones, a COK parishioner, Mr. Charles Way, CEO of the Beach Company, answered the need. He made available the vacated Jaber's Market building at 739 Coleman Boulevard, where the Boulevard Condominiums are today. This relocated distribution center went into full-scale operation on September 30, 1989, and continued until November 15, 1989.

The following is a diary from Sister deLourdes, who was responsible for the day-to-day operations. I've only included the first fourteen days.

DAYS OF RECOVERY ...
BEGINNINGS OF ECCO

THURS., SEPT. 21, 1989: Hurricane Hugo blew over Charleston in the very early hours of the morning.

FRI. SEPT. 22 – **DAY 1**

SAT. SEPT. 23 – **DAY 2**: 7 p.m. curfew in Mount Pleasant

SUN. SEPT. 24 – **DAY 3**: *Post & Courier* published picture after picture of devastation/continuing to do so for days to come. People really came out for church today.

MON. SEPT. 25 – **DAY 4**: Gather emergency phone numbers (that will keep changing). The only working phone was in a rectory closet. That's where we began. 1st look at Sullivan's Island by residents/by boat. Father Carter met with area ministers trying to get central location for outreach program. RAIN! RAIN! RAIN!

TUES. SEPT. 26 – **DAY 5**: COK food distribution begins from parish hall. Days on the job are 7 a.m.–9:30 p.m. Water is safe to drink in most areas now.

WED. SEPT. 27 – **DAY 6**: East Cooper ministers meet at Christ Our King. I gave a report on what we're doing and what we know at this point. Islands are closed.

THURS. SEPT. 28 – **DAY 7**: Over 20 trucks of food have come in. Gailliard Center gave us 3 vans of supplies. Serving up to 400 families daily. 200 volunteers (20 daily) to help in this 3 week period.

FRI. SEPT. 29 – **DAY 8**: Helpers came from out of town to help clean up, chain saw, etc. Sullivan's Island residents over 16 yrs old may return to homes between 9 a.m. & 5 p.m. Ferry from Shem Creek/free/must have ID, bring food & water. Private boats allowed. Materials for emergency repairs will be distributed. Volunteers to help must be 16 yrs old. Water in bad shape now … raw sewage on Coleman Blvd. Pressure down/Begging folks to use very little.

SAT. SEPT. 30 – **DAY 9**: COK & Stella Maris parishes all worship at COK together. Stella Maris operates out of COK office & church bldg. Food distribution moves to vacant Jaber's store on Coleman Blvd.

SUN. OCT. 1 – **DAY 10**: Curfew in Mount Pleasant these days Sept 22–Oct. 15.

MON. OCT. 2 – **DAY 11**: John Woods from Atlanta brought a case of Post-it notes. And I believe he was responsible for the Motorola walkie-talkies + 4 cell phones. Ben Sawyer bridge to reopen after repairs (NOT)—Delayed! Things seem to get calmer around Christ Our King. Father Evatt took us to dinner at AW Shucks at 8:30 p.m. Real HOT food for the second time since Hugo. Returned home late to find electricity at my home too. So nice to have some semblance of NORMAL life again.

TUES. OCT. 3– **DAY 12**: People are now beginning to come/tell about their homes gone. NEW PHASE of Hugo. Father Carter & I rode to Copahee—returned to find lights & electricity at rectory.

WED. OCT. 4 – **DAY 13**: Oprah today at 4 p.m.— King St. Palace. J. Conick (Catholic Banner) looking to create an article for Oct.12 issue. Need a phone desperately at Jaber's. It's quite an operation.

THURS. OCT. 5 – **DAY 14**: Workers coming from away … area outside COK hall is prepared for them— tents, water for showers, etc. Hibben Methodist Church looking for help to purchase, cook, feed 20 Mennonites one day 2wks. Jan Maize—COK key person. Sullivan's Island Baptist to use COK parish hall for services

FRI. OCT. 6 – **DAY 15**: Father James Carter (by phone): "Continue what we're doing."

Del Bene, who worked as the medical director of the hospitals at the Medical University of South Carolina at the time Hugo struck, remembers the early use of the center quite well:

Initially the new center served as many as four hundred persons a day. Later the center functioned on weekends only. Many of the volunteers had returned to work and were not available on weekdays. Mrs. Carol Robinson, a volunteer from Aiken, South Carolina, took over the direction of the relocated distribution center from Connie Dopierala. She coordinated truck deliveries, the unloading and stocking of supplies, and supervised the volunteers. When needed, she also handed out supplies.

Although Del Bene's responsibilities in the disaster response were to secure the patient care operations of the hospitals, ensuring that all the buildings and staff were in place for the hospitals to provide health care during the days that followed the hurricane, after work he would come to the makeshift response location and unload eighteen-wheelers from across the country.

CHRISTIAN ACTION PROGRAM

Around mid-October, less than a month after Hugo, ministers from several church communities met at the COK church. They discussed the feasibility of a Christian Action Program, a program that would transform the emergency response movement into an ongoing effort to alleviate poverty in the area east of the Cooper. The needy from each congregation would receive vouchers that could then be redeemed at the Jaber's Market for food, clothing, and other necessities.

The ministers at the meeting were asked to continue parts of the relief program within their church communities. At the same time, they were asked to join together to come up with a plan that would answer the Gospel mandate (to feed the hungry, clothe the naked, give drink to the thirsty, and care for the sick) in the communities.

[The plan included a] voucher system [that] offered a twofold value. It would help screen those in need of immediate assistance. At the same time, the system would lead to additional plans for various types of professional assistance later.

The first building ECCO used, The Old Jabber's Market on Coleman Blvd. After complaints were received by adjoining tenants, a new building was found.

JOINT EFFORT SERVED THOUSANDS

About one week after Hugo struck (in late September) and until the first of December, thousands of needy folks had been served. At peak, three hundred to four hundred families were being served each day at the temporary distribution center.

Christ Our King assumed the food distribution efforts. Sullivan's Island Baptist, Hibben United Methodist, and St. Paul's Lutheran churches handled the distribution of clothing.

As normalcy began to return to Mount Pleasant, tenants of the stores near the Jaber's Market complained that truck deliveries and the great numbers of persons using the facility adversely affected their businesses. They requested that the relief effort be closed or relocated. So the relief effort was moved back to Christ Our King for a few months and operated out of several rented containers situated on Russell Drive, the main street that led to the church.

CATHOLIC DIOCESE DISASTER-RESPONSE EFFORT

Bishop Coadjutor, the Most Reverend David B. Thompson, led the Catholic Diocese of Charleston disaster-response effort. The diocese made available $1 million for immediate relief. Bishop Thompson used this money to aid the needy individuals and families of the diocese.

With funding from the Bishop and from the National Catholic Disaster Relief Committee of Catholic Charities, the parishes of Stella Maris and Christ Our King provided assistance to hundreds of families in the area. About fourteen thousand families received $1,000 or less; about a hundred families received $1,000 to $5,000, and approximately fifty received $5,000 to $10,000. Most of these moneys went to repair houses and automobiles and to replace home furnishings and equipment.

* * *

As stated in a 1990 ECCO brochure: "Just as the winds of Hugo cleared sections of trees and created new vistas, they also swept away the blinders of our complacency that permitted the needs of so many in our area to go unaddressed."

* * *

PROPOSAL FOR CHRISTIAN ACTION PROJECT

In mid-October of 1989, Sister deLourdes prepared a proposal to be discussed at meetings with pastors from churches where the voucher system was to be used. The stated goal of the project was "To establish a Christian-action project that focuses on post-hurricane disaster assistance for economically disadvantaged persons in the East Cooper area (e.g., Hamlin Beach, Copahee, and Awendaw)."

Objectives of the project included the establishment of the following:

- a food distribution center

- a clothing and household goods distribution center

- a center that would provide short-term assistance to secure adequate housing, to find jobs, to acquire legal assistance, and to create a system that would refer those in need to appropriate community agencies for specific problems (e.g., health-related concerns, nutrition, and counseling)

HUGO RELIEF COMMITTEE LEADING TO ECCO

During the latter months of 1989 and early months of 1990, the Hugo Relief Committee of Christ Our King Parish and a newly created steering committee (of the fledgling organization that would become ECCO) began to analyze the planning and fund-raising required to meet the goal of establishing the Christian-action project.

A three-phase proposal was set forth as the second generation of relief efforts at COK Parish became operational. The main elements of the plan were to:

- document immediate needs and access available resources;

- provide training and stress management for "caretakers," i.e., responders to the grassroots immediate physical needs;

- hire a full-time co-coordinator;

- help the St. Vincent de Paul Society provide monetary assistance and disseminate relief donations;

- redirect excess supplies and donations to other needy places (some shipped to Puerto Rico for victims of Hugo); and

- participate in building community, by working together with churches and social service agencies.

Applications for grants to support the project were submitted to the National Catholic Disaster Relief Committee and Trident Community Foundation. The original application referred to the project as the Cooper Area Relief Effort, or C.A.R.E. It indicated that the C.A.R.E. Center would serve as the focal point for coordinating people and programs to "decrease the frustration of persons being sent from one place to another."

ADMINISTERING C.A.R.E.

Fund-raising letters from ECCO written in April 1990 explained that, in addition to goods and services, $100,000 had been distributed in the Hugo relief effort east of the Cooper River. The effort had tapped into additional services that provided mobile homes and connected needy families to those wanting to adopt a family. That year, Thanksgiving and Christmas dinners were provided to those in need, with the outreach project playing Santa to more than a hundred families.

DIMINISHING COMPASSION AND ASSISTANCE

It was at this point that Father Carter noted that the momentum of human compassion was diminishing and that federal and state assistance was drying up. He indicated that plans were under way to launch the second generation of the relief effort. This would involve the establishment of a permanent distribution center for all of the East Cooper area. An established relief center would act as a magnet to attract agencies and organizations that served the poor to coordinate the volunteers to provide that help.

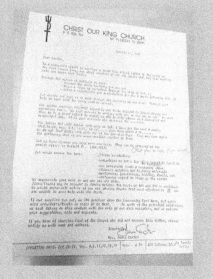

He sought money from donors to help open a new building, where supplies would be collected and distributed. Volunteers would come to the new center to help distribute building supplies, food, and household items. Additional space at the center would house volunteers who would offer legal assistance and social-service referrals and provide a link to federal, state, and local agencies.

Later, the center could add literacy training while seeking assistance from other area churches.

In his letter, Father Carter referred to the center as ECCO.

THE FIRST CENTER

With assistance from Mount Pleasant mayor, Dick Jones, a four-thousand-square foot building was located (to house the center) at 870 North Lansing Drive in Mount Pleasant next door to the National Guard Armory.

This builidng on Lansing Drive was ECCO's home for almost fourteen years.

This new center included a small suite of offices on the first floor, a warehouse, and a loft, which provided additional meeting space.

ECCO'S FIRST BUDGET

The first budget for ECCO was dated February 1990. It included a request for funds from South Carolina's governor, Carroll Campbell.

The proposed budgeted amount was $252,460. This included capital expenditures of:

- $197,000 for a building, equipment, and renovations;

- $28,000 for a director and coordinator;

- $7,700 for supplies (bulk of food to be donated); and

- $15,260 for contracted services (half of that for utilities), insurance, etc.

Monsignor Carter discovered that an unrealized population of the poor and needy existed in the church's backdoor community, and his compassion led churches to respond.

A year later in 1990, a community investigation of needed health services was conducted. Dental services were the most urgent unmet need; studies show that poor oral hygiene leads to tooth decay, and infected teeth can lead to heart disease and diabetes. A single-wide trailer was secured and placed on the ECCO property beside the small warehouse facility. A dental chair was installed to provide emergency tooth extractions for the working poor; abscessed teeth were removed at no cost to the recipient.

In 2000, ECCO launched a prescription assistance program to help supply the poor with prescriptions they could not afford. Stories emerged of people taking half or less of their prescribed dosages because they were on fixed incomes. Emergency medications were provided to patients referred by physicians who knew those patients could not afford to pay for the medications prescribed to them. These consisted of anything from antibiotics to statins to diabetic medications. Patients who needed prescriptions for ongoing chronic needs like hypertension and diabetes were assisted in making application to pharmaceutical companies. This program continues to assist hundreds of clients who otherwise would not be able to afford their medication.

In late 2003, ECCO built and moved into a new fourteen-thousand-square-foot building debt-free, made possible in part by a generous memorial gift from the estate of Donald Barhyte, a member of the Christ Our King parish. Barhyte, a Florida resident, was a friend of Monsignor Carter. He named the beneficiary of this portion of his estate in memory of his wife Pat. When it opened, according to Del Bene and Galasso, "the facility contained a state-of-the-art dental clinic, a warehouse for food and clothing storage and distribution, warehouse and distribution space for the Saint Vincent de Paul organization's furniture collection and distribution, teaching/meeting spaces, and counseling cubicles." Today, the building houses a state-of-the-art dental clinic, a medical office, staff offices, meeting rooms, and more than five thousand square feet of storage for food, clothing, and furniture. Later chapters in this book have more information about the new building.

Donald Barhyte

ECCO's main building

The entire cost of land was given by a generous benefactor. The building itself was provided by a gift of $750,000 from the estate of Floridian Donald S. Barhyte in memory of his wife Pat. To make the funding complete, ECCO added another $250,000 from the sale of the original building.

ADVANCING THE MISSION

The second capital fund-raiser, "Advancing the Mission," began in 2004 [and raised] $1.3 million dollars ... for building renovations, disaster relief, and basic operations (the goal was $1.2 million). This achievement allowed ECCO to begin catalyzing a community grassroots disaster-preparedness strategy and involvement of the community in defining future initiatives. The funds led to space renovation, which allowed inclusion of the Catholic Charity Immigration Center. Later, unused space was configured in partnership with the Medical University of South Carolina (MUSC) into a medical office to house a family medicine practice and a free emergency medical clinic (C.A.R.E. Clinic). Further refinements to the 2003 building allowed space for private counseling rooms, a teaching classroom, and computer-based education classrooms.

In 2008, a shift began in the strategy for helping the poor. In prior years, assistance was given with no intention of helping the client any further. ECCO was just "giving fish away." The client was only being sustained in their current situation. That strategy changed in 2008 to "teaching people to fish." Education and programs had to be implemented to make this happen.

DON'T GIVE FISH ... TEACH TO FISH

The thrust of ECCO's response to the community it serves has evolved over the years. ECCO's excellent and dependable support services continue to provide safety net services for all of our clients. ECCO now provides programs, which help those who want to move up and out of poverty. That initiative, begun in 2007, has led to services and partnerships that help individuals succeed in improving their situation. ECCO provides a case management and counseling program in support of individuals aspiring to help themselves. ECCO provides intensive and individualized dental care, including dentures; ongoing private, free medical care through the nurse practitioner program; counseling on job readiness and job management; and financial and computer literacy education. ECCO has partnership arrangements to help clients earn a GED diploma and apply for employment. ECCO facilitates job placement through established connections with regional employers.

It's extremely rewarding to see how a nonprofit can be more effective and efficient in serving and providing the tools for the less fortunate to use in following their personal goals and visions resulting in their becoming financially independent.

The history continues into the present and the future; I have been extremely fortunate to be a part of this by being at the right place at the right time and following the leadership from above.

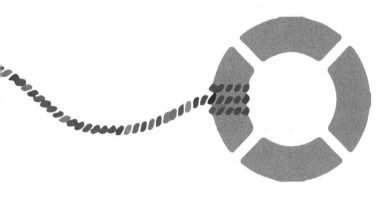

CHAPTER 2
Rural vs. Urban

A s we focus in on ECCO and its story, it's important to understand that the organization serves a primarily rural area in our 1,500 square miles. There is a distinct difference between rural and urban poverty, and in this chapter we need to understand the difference because I have worked in both arenas.

From 1985 to 1991, I served in rural Hall County, Georgia, located in the pastoral foothills of the Appalachian Mountains forty miles northeast of Atlanta. The county was known for having more mobile homes than any other county in the state— and twice as many as the county in second place in the rankings. In 1991, I relocated to urban Charleston, South Carolina.

Moving from Gainesville, Georgia, to Charleston was an eye-opening experience. The total population in Hall County, where Gainesville is the county seat, was just over ninety thousand, compared with Charleston's population of over six hundred thousand, including the metro area, North Charleston, and many other communities. The numbers themselves speak volumes, but needless to say, there were many differences in the settings, so I knew the methods of work had to change to meet the opportunities in a metropolitan area. Gainesville had one housing project in the city limits. Charleston, combined with North Charleston, has more than twenty. The most obvious difference was the density in the housing communities. Gainesville had multitudes of mobile home parks where the homes were spaced out with small yards. The concentration of population in Charleston is much more dense, which I discovered brings higher rates of violence, theft, and drugs. There was such a drastic difference, I knew I needed to readjust and develop a new strategy.

Charleston County is mostly an urban area—the second-largest populated county in the state and the state's most-populated metropolitan area. To the north, lower Berkeley County, a very rural expanse, is larger than the state of Rhode Island.

When I worked with the Charleston Baptist Association, my focus mainly centered on the urban communities in most of Charleston's and North Charleston's housing projects; we started working with those residents at that time. I also worked extensively with migrant workers on rural Johns Island.

There are similarities but also huge differences in serving the poor and working poor in a rural community versus an urban community, and understanding the differences between rural and urban poverty is essential to creating successful ministries and programs.

The most obvious difference in the poor in a rural area is that its residents are dispersed across a larger geographical area. This fact brings on many challenges for the rural poor, with the primary challenge being the lack of access to resources. Although social agencies, soup kitchens, and homeless shelters are more prevalent in urban communities, urban poverty-laden communities have a dense population, which brings on a unique set of challenges.

As is often the case with rural communities, rural poverty is often cast in the shadow of urban and suburban issues. Yet, one in five Americans lives in a rural area, and a higher share of rural residents live in poverty compared to urban residents (14 percent of rural residents versus 11 percent of urban residents).[1]

When most people think of poverty, the focus tends to be on inner-city poverty because of the high density of the population. Urban poverty—with all of its crime and welfare issues—is portrayed much more regularly in the news, which draws attention to the huge lack of resources. Groups and organizations focus on these overwhelming challenges because the needs are so great. These communities dwarf the needs of rural poverty, and the needs are much more evident when driving through these neighborhoods. They're the kind of places where we all lock our doors as we pass through out of uncertainty and fear because of a reputation for problems.[2]

Communities in rural areas have many distinct characteristics that most people don't recognize. Access to resources, transportation, economic structures, institutions, and educational

---

1 "Place Matters: Addressing Rural Poverty," Rural Research Policy Institute, April 2004, accessed September 2, 2015, http://www.rupri.org/Forms/synthesis.pdf.

2 Fagan, Patrick. "The Real Root Causes of Violent Crime: The Breakdown of Marriage, Family, and Community," The Heritage Foundation, March 17, 1995, accessed September 2, 2015, http://www.heritage.org/research/reports/1995/03/bg1026nbsp-the-real-root-causes-of-violent-crime.

institutions is limited. In rural East Cooper, grocery stores can be as far as twenty-five miles away. Public transportation runs on a very limited basis. Besides travel by automobile, public transportation is limited to a bus system made up of the Charleston Area Regional Transportation Authority (CARTA) and Tri-county Link. CARTA provides a comprehensive plan for those in the nearby community, but transfers to connect with other routes can be very time consuming. For example, a student who attends our technical college by public transportation for half a day has to be allowed time to get to the campus. The rural system, Tri-county Link, serves the outlying area with only two trips per day for our area in Charleston County, but none connect lower Berkeley County with our community, making the college inaccessible by public transportation for residents of lower Berkeley County. Tri-county Link serves only the most populated areas and major highways. Visits to doctor's offices, social agencies, or even banks are major challenges.

I realized that understanding the causes of poverty creates a better opportunity to address how and why it exists in our country. Hearing noted educator and author Ruby Payne speak on the root causes of poverty enlightened me in spite of my years of experience. It was like not seeing the forest for the trees; I had never stepped back to see poverty from a quantitative perspective. But I was ready and eager to learn.

It's also important to see how government services differ in these areas as well. In the rural areas, services are rarely available compared to the urban communities.

There are many theories that define the causes of persistent rural poverty. For simplicity, we will focus on three:

1. The human capital theory, which contends that people are poor because they do not have the educational opportunities and work skills to obtain good-paying jobs

2. The economic organization theory, which maintains that poverty results from a lack of job opportunities

3. The culture-of-poverty theory, where human action is both constrained and enabled by the choices and actions of the individual

These dynamics are important to our understanding of the production and reproduction of poverty and social inequality. Individual choices tend to follow family habits and patterns.

HUMAN CAPITAL THEORY— JOBS AND EDUCATION

The poor in rural communities lack opportunity to the educational and employment advantages that those in urban communities have. Adding to that problem are the generational customs that have been passed down and accepted as the norm. South Carolina Governor Nikki Haley made a commitment in her 2015 inaugural address to recruit more highly trained and qualified teachers in the state's rural areas. Teachers are much less likely to locate to a rural area to work and live. This is due to the slow pace of life, lower salaries, and lack of opportunities to be effective in their work.

A study conducted by Huang and Van Horn (1995) found that rural educators find much more resistance to change and remediation from the children in rural compared to urban settings due to predetermination, passivity, and religious reasons that are far more ingrained in rural cultures than urban ones.[3] Change in rural communities does not come quickly.

When I came to Charleston, I recognized that rural communities are made up of many smaller communities. For instance, the small fishing village of McClellanville has nine different communities. The total population was 499 in the 2010 census. Each community has its own unique hierarchy system, including a leader/maven that residents look to for guidance and leadership. Developing trust with others outside of the community, no matter how small, historically has been an issue and still is today. Having communities, especially residents of heirs' property, unite and come to consensus on a policy or initiative is very challenging, as each community has its own priorities and agendas.

In coming to East Cooper, I learned of a new type of property, heirs' property.

In the Lowcountry of South Carolina, heirs' property (HP) is mostly rural land owned by African Americans who either purchased or were deeded land after the Civil War. Historically, HP owners were routinely denied access to the legal system, could not afford to pay for legal services, and didn't understand or trust the legal system. As a result, much of this land was passed down through the generations without the benefit of a written will, or the will was not probated within the ten years required by

---

3 Stansell, Amanda, and T.F., McLaughlin, "A Brief Comparison of Rural Poverty and Urban Poverty at its Consequences for Students with Special Needs," International Journal of Basics and Applied Sciences 1, no. 3 (2013): 587–593

South Carolina law to make it valid—so the land became heirs' property.

Often the family members didn't know that.

Heirs' property is land owned "in common" (known as tenants in common) by all of the heirs, regardless of whether they live on the land, pay the taxes, or have never set foot on the land. These are often referred to as settlement communities.

Why is this a risky way to own land?

Heirs' property ownership is risky because the land can be easily lost. Any heir can sell his/her percentage of ownership to another, who can force a sale of the entire property in the courts.[4]

Another significant difference between urban and rural poverty is in the education of the parents, which is lower than that of urban parents. Rural residents are less likely to have strong academic backgrounds and may not have graduated from high school. For example, 18 percent of rural parents living in poverty had a college education compared to 25 percent of urban parents living in poverty. High school graduation rates have indicated that only 13 percent of the urban parents did not graduate high school whereas 19 percent of the rural parents living in poverty did not graduate. Also, parents in rural areas have less of an understanding

---

4 "What is Heirs' Property?" Center for Heirs' Property Preservation, accessed September 2, 2015, http://www.heirsproperty.org/who-we-are/what-is-heirs-property.

of the educational criteria required of their children than parents in urban communities.[5]

When entering the first grade, children living in poverty are usually two years behind their classmates. They are behind in their reading, writing, and arithmetic. Social and behavioral skills are lacking as well. This is in part due to the lack of education for their parents and/or the parents working two or three jobs in trying to make ends meet. Growing up in a rural area amplifies the extreme challenges of this population, and recognizing this point is crucial for the development of an educated and skilled workforce.

Students attending schools in rural communities have far fewer resources, and qualified teachers are harder to employ. Rural teachers have to perform multiple roles in the community in a relatively small environment, whereas urban educators, though they may serve multiple roles in a community, are operating in a much bigger environment and have an easier time keeping all of those roles separate.

ECONOMIC ORGANIZATION THEORY—JOB OPPORTUNITIES

Rural workers are also at a disadvantage because manufacturing companies and corporate headquarters tend to settle in urban areas. Job opportunities in rural areas are very limited, and those that are available are typically unskilled; that factor, combined with little or no competition for employees, means employers that are located in these communities can offer lower wages and

5 Huang, Gary and Patricia Van Hom, "Using child care services: Families with disabled children in nonmetropolitan areas," Rural Special Education Quarterly, Fall 1995, 14(4), 27–36.

provide little prospect of career advancement. There are few, if any, summer job programs, and the few year-round jobs that do exist tend to be temporary work positions, leading to underemployment. When there are more employers in a rural community, wages and demands for labor increase as the businesses compete for available workers. These circumstances perpetuate the state of rural poverty. I applaud Governor Nikki Haley for her successful efforts in recruiting new industry in our state's rural communities. In March 2012, Haley said, "It's a great day in South Carolina! There is more work to be done, but we are moving in a great direction."

These are some of the rural businesses and corporations located in our state: LowCountry Biomass LLC expanded Jasper County facility; Nexans established a cable plant in Berkeley County, creating two hundred new jobs; Tognum America Inc. expanded in Aiken County; Rolled Alloys established new operations in Chester County, creating twenty-four new jobs; Caterpillar expanded in Sumter County, creating eighty new jobs; Naturally Advanced Technologies Inc. established a new facility in Florence County, creating twenty-five new jobs; Belk Inc. established a new distribution center in Union County, creating 124 new jobs; Jones-Hamilton chose Chester County for a new plant, creating new jobs; GSE Lining Technology expanded in Williamsburg County.

The majority of jobs in ECCO's service area are related to the tourism industry. Therefore, the wages paid are hourly and are generally low. Restaurants and hotels require low-skilled labor to do the majority of work. In the food and beverage industry, busboys, servers, dishwashers, and cooks earn little because the supply of labor is greater than the demand. The same holds true for jobs in the hotel/hospitality industry, where most of the available positions are in groundskeeping, housekeeping, and maintenance. Sales staff members are young professionals and are paid as entry-level positions.

Compounding the challenge is the fact that business owners and agency leaders are not typically residents of these rural communities. Those few who are residents bring their personal involvement and resources—valuable assets such as dollars, influence, and personal contacts.

CULTURE OF POVERTY THEORY—LEARNED BEHAVIORS

Most rural people tend to follow the habits and patterns of daily living that have been passed down through their families for generations. When offering new ideas in money spending, family relationships, employment practices, and so on, it is vital to remember that rural people have seen their own practices sustain (good or not) their families for a long time. Behavior is a result of personal good and bad history and the patterns of parents and extended family.

In the beginning days in Gainesville, my responsibility was to interview those looking for financial assistance. I interviewed all kinds of people, including one who claimed she was the Messiah and a man who had just been released from prison. One of my biggest weaknesses was for a homeless family living in their car. My wife and I had just birthed our first child, and I would tear up hearing these stories, knowing their innocent babies and young children were suffering as well.

I recall a man who came in and was recently released from prison. He had nothing but the clothes on his back. I took him home for lunch that day and kept in touch with him by having periodic phone calls and lunches. I was surprised one day when I went to the local prison for our monthly service. He was there, sitting in the congregation, and I went up to him and asked, "What are you doing here?" out of my surprise for seeing him after he had just been released. He truly wanted to change.

Many of these people were taken under my wing. But the one I remember most was a lady named Vicki who left her husband because he was beating her. He had beaten her the night before she showed up with her two children at our office asking for financial assistance, and she was scared for her life. Her immediate need was food and temporary housing, so we gave her food and found housing in a local housing community. But she also needed to move away from Dahlonega by the weekend, and she had no way to move her things and no one to help her.

Convinced of her story, I rented a U-Haul and showed up bright and early Saturday morning to take her to her new place in a Section 8 housing community in Gainesville. She still struggled. She couldn't get a job, because she had to take care of her young children. And shortly after she relocated, her car was repossessed, so we bought her a new gently used one from an auction.

During my time working with her, I learned her mother was an alcoholic and her dad was in prison. When a mother lives a life of dependency, relying on food pantries and emergency rental or housing assistance from different nonprofits around the city, then the child grows up believing that same mode of living— surviving crisis to crisis—is the norm: "Since this got my mother by, what's wrong with me doing it, too? It was good enough for her so it should be for me," the child may think. After working with Vicki, I began to understand that her pattern of behavior was learned from her mother; she had to have a crisis to survive, and she had to have someone pulling her through. I knew she needed more in-depth help than I could offer. This experience spawned my thoughts for developing a more complete response in breaking the cycle of poverty learned from prior generations. The need of a young mother's class for empowerment and a job readiness program registered as well.

Another example of learned behavior was the father who quit his job because his boss said something negative to him or about him. "Nobody talks to me like that!" he says. So when his son or daughter grows up and gets a job, they have the same response. Their boss says something and the child walks off the job. "I got too much pride. Nobody talks to me like that," the child will echo. These negative practices have been so deeply engrained in their lives that when put in the same situation, they respond in the same way as their parent. It's a delicate matter when a person (social worker, teacher, or volunteer) offers an alternative way of living, which they may find offensive.

Thinking about habits repeated from previous generations reminds me of the story about the grandmother cooking a roast. A little girl asks her mother, "Why do you cut the ends off of the roast and throw them away?" The mom says, "Why, that's the way my mother always did it." So the little girl grows up learning to throw away the ends of the roast until, as a new bride, her husband questions the practice. The next time the family gathers at the grandmother's house for a meal, the question is posed to the grandmother: "Why do you cut off the ends of the roast and throw them away?" The grandmother replies, "I did that because the pan wasn't big enough." So often the culture of poverty comes from the lineage of family traditions.

NEIGHBORHOODS AND NETWORKS

Another difference between urban and rural poverty is the makeup of the geographic or spatial areas they encompass. Urban communities are known to have local neighborhoods that are made up of a very defined area, a square mile or two, whereas rural communities may have neighborhoods that spread over several miles. In an urban neighborhood, residents may or may not know their neighbors. There is commonly a higher turnover among those who live in urban areas—people move in and out—and the frequent turnover makes the residents oblivious to the comings and goings of the people on their street.

Rural neighborhoods are different. Even though the population is not as dense, the sense of community is much stronger. Tenure is much more long term, as families may live there for generations; it is not unusual for children reared in a rural community to remain there for their lifetime. Residents know where their friends and neighbors live, what kind of car they drive, and which cars are supposed to be in which neighbor's driveway. When they are in need of something, they ask for their neighbors' help.

Recently, I was in a meeting about opening a ministry satellite site in a rural community twenty miles from our center. We were discussing how to get the programming and scheduling information to the residents of the community. One of the attending committee members, who was a pastor in that community, told us that the residents communicate often with each other because of the close family bonds. Most have been linked to the same families for generations. When something happens, they are immediately on the phone with each other, reporting what they have learned. He recalled traveling home from out of town and receiving a call about the death of a church member. When he got back into his community, he passed by the home of the deceased, and the driveway and yard were full of the cars of church members and community neighbors. "They all found out before I got there!" the pastor said.

When we were meeting with the community about opening the satellite, which would be located at the end of a dead end road, some of the residents were concerned about the increase of traffic on their street. They told us they knew every car that traveled up and down their street. When they didn't recognize a car, they would call the other neighbors on the street to see if they could identify who it was. Their network carried on day and night!

POVERTY AND CHILDREN

East Cooper is home to the very wealthy and the very poor. The poverty is hidden; one can drive for miles and see nothing but upper middle class housing. But dirt roads and driveways intersect with these same roads, and these indicate where the poor live. They are routes to the heirs' property or settlement communities mentioned earlier—some of the most common pockets of deep poverty. There may be twenty or thirty homes down these access roads. In fact, in Mount Pleasant alone there are twelve different communities called heirs' property or settlement communities. In lower Berkeley County, eighteen exist.

Many of the people we help in the South will never be home-owners because they live on heirs' property. Having assets is a key component that separates the financially stable from those who are financially dependent. Becoming financially stable begins with home ownership.

Heirs' property is very common in East Cooper. One might see a very poor family living in a shanty and a family living in a $500,000 home on the same property. A lot of the massive growth we have in East Cooper is due to the sellout by out-of-town family members who may have never lived or visited the property but who signed over their rights to ownership to a developer. In fact, heirs' property covers most of our service area.

Two separate needs surveys have been conducted in our service area. In 2010 we worked extensively with the Mount Pleasant settlement leaders. In 2014, another survey was taken in the Cainhoy/Wando/Huger area. Both surveys included more than thirty communities, and home repair was in the top three needs in each of these areas. But many of the homes badly in need of repair were located on heirs' property. Many of the families living in these homes applied for repairs to be made, but their requests could not be answered, because they had no title to the property they resided on. After we referred one home to a sister nonprofit, we visited the property and realized it was on heirs' property, which meant the funding would not cover the repairs since the home must be owned by the occupant and a title must be produced.

Deep poverty is commonly defined as having cash income below half of one's poverty threshold.[6] In 2012, according to the federal government guidelines on poverty, deep poverty is a subsistence level of less than $27,890 annually for a family of four.[7] As with overall poverty, deep poverty among children is more acute in rural areas (12.2 percent) than in urban areas (the national average is 9.2 percent according to World Vision, a Christian humanitarian organization). Not only are deep poverty rates among children higher than those for the overall population, but children in deep poverty have experienced higher rates of growth over the last decade, particularly in rural areas. While the 2012 rural/urban gaps in both total and deep poverty are not as large as they were in the 1980s, estimates indicate that, with child poverty increasing in rural areas in 2010–2012 and urban child poverty declining, rural/urban gaps in child poverty may yet reach their mid-1980s levels.[8]

Emotional affects are seen in those who have been raised in poverty. Children in impoverished environments do not have the opportunity for training nor do they have access to adequate

6 Rosmann, Michael, "USDA says poverty increasing in rural America," Farm & Ranch Guide, May 28, 2014, accessed September 3, 2015, http://www.farman-dranchguide.com/entertainment/country_living/farm_and_ranch_life/usda-says-poverty-increasing-in-rural-america/article_4f2094b8-e6a4-11e3-a463-0019bb2963f4.html.

7 Office of The Assistant Secretary for Planning and Evaluation, US Department of Health and Human Services.

8 Rosmann, Michael, "USDA says poverty increasing in rural America," Farm & Ranch Guide, May 28, 2014, accessed September 3, 2015, http://www.farman-dranchguide.com/entertainment/country_living/farm_and_ranch_life/usda-says-poverty-increasing-in-rural-america/article_4f2094b8-e6a4-11e3-a463-0019bb2963f4.html.

intellectual stimulation or health care. Poverty negatively impacts the cognitive ability in children during the early developmental years, with the most significant effects of poverty potentially occurring during the early childhood years (birth to age five). Children in persistent poverty for four or more years ultimately direct more actions outward toward others. These actions include physical aggression, destruction of property, underage drinking, and running away from home, along with problematic behaviors that are directed toward the self. A lot of these actions come from negative self-esteem. Long-term poverty has a greater negative impact on children's cognitive ability than short-term poverty. However, the long-term cognitive effect (into the teen years) still lacks a solid research base to make any accurate conclusions.[9]

Again, parents often are either overwhelmed by working two or three jobs to make ends meet or unacquainted with how to work developmentally with their child. In essence, the parents do not spend time with their children to nurture their growth and maturity.

In addition to creating lasting learning and behavioral problems, early poverty leads to health problems. Inadequate education regarding health and nutritional needs often results in undernutrition or malnutrition among the rural poor.

Rural children are more likely to be poor, and poverty is more likely to be enduring and persistent in their community. Because of resources available to the urban community, the inner-city child has many more opportunities to elevate himself or herself out of poverty than the poor child in rural America. Urban children have mass transit, jobs, access to role models who can

9 Stansell, Amanda, and T.F., McLaughlin (2013).

provide mentoring opportunities, and educational systems with better resources.

In a blog post from October 5, 2015, about reducing poverty in rural communities, the Annie E. Casey Foundation states:

> About 1.5 million children in rural areas—which tend to be more isolated from key resources—live in poverty. The rural child poverty rate consistently exceeds the rate for urban kids and has been on the rise since 2008. In addition, about 80 percent of the nation's counties with persistent child poverty—that is, with rates of at least 20 percent over the past three decades—are rural.

But while children in the city have more available resources than those who live in the country, they also have to deal with more danger—through potential exposure to illegal activities and opportunities to participate in them.

The high concentration of urban residents causes tensions to be higher among them. The knowledge and practice of negotiation skills are limited at best. Consequently, disagreements often result in violence. Drugs and gangs are much more common in urban communities.

In spite of the fact that rural children do not have the luxury of mentoring opportunities, many of them appear to be happier; they have had limited exposure to wealth, luxuries, and modern conveniences, so they don't truly realize that they are poor. Seldom do they see luxurious cars, fancy restaurants, current fashion trends, or even the latest technology; therefore, their current situation becomes more acceptable as a way of life. They are happy with the status quo.

Taking a step back, we need to realize the difference this makes in early childhood education. Recently in Charleston, a group of concerned citizens called "Cradle to Career" has begun addressing the lack of early childhood development and prenatal care. When a child from poverty enters the first grade, records indicate they are two to three years behind their peers from more affluent backgrounds. The advocacy group is making an attempt to solve the dilemma of children lagging behind in the early primary years in the tri-county area.

Prenatal and infant death are two areas that have been a concern; it's so unnecessary for these early deaths to occur in a country as advanced as ours. But in coming to Charleston, I realized that South Carolina has the highest infant mortality rate of all fifty states and that the highest rate in the state is in this region. To examine this issue, in 2009 we asked the Medical University of South Carolina (MUSC), our collaborative partner that has a family practice in our building, to record the number of women from our service area who came to its emergency room to deliver babies without having had any prenatal care—these women had never seen a doctor during their pregnancy. Over the period of one year, the number recorded was fifty-one; it is expected that their prenatal care was minimal at best. No records were kept to determine the health of the newborn, nor was there any longitudinal following to determine how the children developed. It is easy to assume that a low number of these children grew up according to the normal standards.

Therefore, it is easy to conclude that a child entering the first grade with this background and these deficiencies would be much more complex.

The ideal solution for these children is to have a nurse or case manager assigned to their low-income families at birth. This professional would educate parents to understand how to nurture the growth of their child. Routine home visits to verify the benchmarks of a developing child would lead to the opportunity of teaching the parent how to read to and edify the child. This is the premise of Parents as Teachers, an international organization whose mission is that all children will learn, grow, and develop to realize their full potential. The organization provides the information, support, and encouragement parents need to help their children develop optimally during the crucial early years of life. Its focus is at-risk children, which includes the poor, children of the incarcerated, and foster children.

In summary, there is a glaring contrast between living in a poor urban neighborhood and living in a place where your entire town is poor. Rural residents have a strong feeling of marginality, helplessness, dependency, and not belonging. They are like aliens in their own country, convinced that the existing institutions do not serve their interests and needs. Along with this feeling of powerlessness is a widespread feeling of inferiority and personal unworthiness.

Poverty is poverty, but there is a difference between the poverty in the city and the poverty in the country. Resources, education, crime, and job opportunities differentiate the two. Also, a person's lifestyle may preclude economic success. In many rural communities, limited opportunities to increase and improve one's skill set inhibit social mobility. Diverse philosophies, plans, and approaches must be utilized to deal with both segments of poverty successfully. These must take into account the root causes of poverty in order to begin to understand and differentiate the two. I saw ECCO's quest to eliminate generational poverty as both a challenge and an opportunity to investigate principles and apply them to these defined variances.

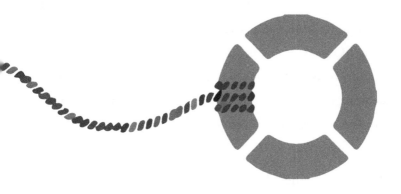

CHAPTER 3
Telling the Story

Telling the community about ECCO is fulfilling for me; I enjoy seeing the message carried to those who have never heard about what we do.

After living in Charleston for more than sixteen years and working in the human services field, I rarely heard anything about ECCO and its ministry. When I arrived at ECCO, my suspicions were confirmed. There was little public awareness of the organization. The story of ECCO had to be told, and I knew how to raise awareness for a program because of my experience at Charleston Outreach, where we had become one of the most visible outreach programs in the country.

Four years prior to my arrival, brochures had been made for a capital campaign to build the current facilities; these were the pride of ECCO's marketing efforts. But at the time of my arrival, I was faced with overcoming the obstacle of no marketing budget.

Experience showed that the best way to tell folks about ECCO was through news stories and advertisements in the local newspapers. While ECCO's story can be shared through many different media outlets, it must be done very deliberately, as it can also be a very delicate story to tell. The best way we've found is to have current and prospective donors visit and tour the facilities and see the activities firsthand.

When I was at the Charleston Baptist Association in 1992, it was a top priority to become familiar with the nonprofits that served the poor in the tri-county area. ECCO was one of the organizations on my list. I set up an appointment with the organization's director. The ECCO warehouse was an old, overcrowded building and needed a lot of work. Marge Del Bene (wife of Victor) said, "The roof leaked from the first day it was occupied until the last day when we moved out."

When I visited, I noticed the atmosphere was very quiet and businesslike. I thought how ECCO was in its own shell battling the world but sheltering itself from it at the same time. In 2005, I responded to an ad in the classifieds. ECCO was seeking an executive director. Weeks went by, and finally I received a phone call from ECCO's search committee inquiring about my interest. I was so excited! I could go back into the field in which God had called me. Before the interview, I became curious and took the initiative to call and set up a tour to visit the organization's facility.

When I arrived, I was surprised to see its new building—it was massive and overwhelming. The spirit and attitude of the staff and volunteers was a stark contrast to what I had seen many years before. It appeared to be an upscale office complex: a 14,000-square-foot building that was less than two years old. This was much different from any other human service nonprofit I had ever seen. All other service organizations I had seen were located in the poorest part of town in old, dilapidated buildings.

When I arrived, I was greeted by Paul Suchy, the volunteer coordinator and warehouse manager, who gave me a tour of the building and facilities.

Eventually, I was selected to take on the leading role at ECCO. I immediately began my efforts to educate the public about the great services and impact that ECCO provided to the community.

The first thing was to get people to see the building and the programs offered. So I began to ask people, especially potential donors, to come and see ECCO's assessable services. At that time, the public's general knowledge of ECCO was that it was a food pantry. Once someone visited and saw that we also offered a myriad of services, I knew we would have their support. Even today they continue to gasp when they visit.

Another great form of exposure was to allow other groups to use ECCO's building for meeting space. Agencies, churches, civic groups, and businesses took us up on the opportunity. The local chapter of ALS, Belk Department Store, and Cracker Barrel have used and continue to use the conference room for employee training.

Right after I arrived at ECCO, a new board member came who was a blessing laid before me. Rod Spaulding was the retired deputy superintendent of Charleston County Schools. He was a prince of a man who was very warm, friendly, and knowledgeable about marketing—an expertise that his past position required.

Rod often joked about his experience in response to bad media coverage of the schools. With his background and knowledge of the media, I knew I could learn a lot.

Rod would come to the office to meet with me and was always astounded by what he saw; ECCO's clients and staff intrigued him. I have always had an open door policy, so when anyone wants to talk or bring a concern to me, I'm there for them. When Spaulding and I would meet in my office, staff would come in and share their situations and dilemmas. He would listen very intently, and when they left, he would say, "Jack, there's a great story." As we walked around the building—throughout the warehouse, staff offices, and lobby—in almost every interaction I had with volunteers, staff, or clients, Rod would always chuckle and say, "Jack, that's another story." I assumed he was just being nice and supportive because that was his nature. But after a several months, I finally asked him, "Rod, why do you keep saying, 'That's another story?'" He replied, "Jack, every person that walks into the building has a story. The way your staff and volunteers help is really impressive. I have never seen anything like it. Y'all do incredible things here for these people who come in here in crises." I finally understood what he was saying. Every encounter is a story, and those stories answer questions about ECCO that loom in the mind of the average person: How do I qualify for ECCO's programs? What happened to that person that they needed to turn to ECCO? How did their problem affect their family? Why does ECCO help these people, and how is it able to do so? The stories tell our story—the story of ECCO.

Rod also taught me to build relationships with the media. He told me, "They are looking for stories. That's their business. They love human interest stories, especially when someone overcomes the hurdles in their life. And just the story of how ECCO started is incredible. ECCO took something bad and made something good out of it." This approach was very enlightening to me.

To help me to better know the media, he took me to meet with the news directors of the local TV stations. He also took me to meet the publishers of our two local weekly papers, Vickey Boyd of the *Moultrie News* and Sue Detar of the *Daniel Island News*, and the publisher of the local paper, the *Post and Courier* newspaper. He made an arrangement with them to publish a monthly column, written by me, in exchange for a paid ad. I had written columns for newsletters in previous positions but never for the paper. It was a new challenge.

The papers told me to write five hundred words, and Rod told me to make them relevant to what ECCO does and advocates. My first submission was in 2007. As a sample, here is my column from January 2015.

WHEN THE WHEELS COME OFF THE BUS

This past summer, my wife, Sue, and I attended one of the summer lecture series at Furman University's Riley Institute. This series was titled, "Can't Win for Losing: The Crisis of the Working Poor." The one we attended was named "Questioning the American Dream: Families and Neighbors Living on the Brink."

When we think of the poor and the working poor, we think as they're always the ones living on the edge, but no income level finds itself exempt from living paycheck to paycheck. It may take you by surprise that many families living in East Cooper live on the brink.

Webster's defines "the brink" as the edge at the top of a steep place. Life's unexpected explosions can divert long-term personal plans and goals. Just one unexpected event can cause a family to go into a financial downward spiral. Reduced work hours, losing a job, unexpected illness, divorce, hospitalization, and a broken down car are some of the multitudinous examples. Once one of these tragic situations is encountered, it is almost impossible for a family to regain the economic stability they once enjoyed. These situations cause many families and individuals to fall over the brink.

Bills continue to arrive as regularly as a heartbeat, and paychecks become irregular. Affordable housing is impossible to find in East Cooper. To rent an average one-bedroom apartment with utilities, a person has to earn more than $19 an hour in a forty-hour work week or work seventy hours a week earning minimum wage of $7.25 an hour. Most of those who work for an hourly wage live in North Charleston or Awendaw because they cannot afford to live in our community due to the high cost of living. Housing is only one of the many expenses they face every day. **This is the plight of the working poor.**

People who need our services are categorized as those who do and do not want to help themselves. Eighty-three percent of the people we serve work and have a job. It's not as if our low-income neighbors aren't working. These folks are trying to get ahead and live responsibly. Many are working two or three jobs and still can't keep up. The pride they exhibit is demonstrated with their hard work in attempting to keep up with the demands of living day to day.

Each month we have around twenty-five new cases that have no prior history of receiving any of our services. The majority of these are in situational poverty. They're in financial crisis. Their crisis may be caused by the many previously mentioned circumstances.

When a client enters our center on Six Mile Road for the first time, they receive a complete, comprehensive assessment with one of our case managers. We look at their immediate need and then analyze the other ongoing needs—like health, dental, employment, and education. The case manager and client work together and devise an individualized plan to better guide the family through their obstacles. Our Financial Assistance program helps a lot of these with rent, utilities, and other albatrosses they unexpectedly find around their necks. Our staff member helps the family determine realistic plans of how to reach their financial goals.

When the wheels come off the bus, ECCO has the tools to help put them back on. We try to exemplify the mercy and compassion of Christ as we meet with each person. Our goal is to strive to help each client reach their greatest potential, guiding individuals toward self-sufficiency and ongoing achievement.

Rod challenged me to write weekly articles for the newspapers, but I didn't have the time to devote; it was all I could do to write one per month. However, his challenge did encourage me to submit a combination of things: news articles, pictures, and my column, which allowed us to have something published three times a month. The focus was to keep ECCO at the forefront of our community. I wanted to make ECCO the "sexy" nonprofit in our community where everyone desired to be involved; everyone would want to be affiliated with ECCO. News stories and testimonials were written about successful clients who made significant advances toward financial independence, significant health goals, or job achievements. We also issued news releases about upcoming classes we were offering.

Today, ECCO has become a favorite nonprofit of the local media. We are one of the most recognized nonprofits in our tri-county area. Each month, we have client stories in the newspaper. Our public relations efforts have grown immensely. In 2014, I gave more responsibility to our director of development, who has done a superb job, and later in the year we began a media relations campaign that encompassed all forms of media, including television commercials on three channels; stories featured in local news outlets; newspaper advertisements, articles, and columns; and even direct mail.

In spite of all of our media efforts, we are surprised that, even today, many people are still unaware of ECCO. We will continue to chisel away at the nearly immovable rock of being unknown while knowing ECCO has a story that people want to hear.

Guess what? Your fifteen-year-old daughter is the proud parent of a brand new baby!

When ECCO embarked on the quest of eliminating poverty in East Cooper communities, we took on a role to educate and inform the general public about what living in poverty is like. In 2009, ECCO acquired the rights to the Community Action Poverty Simulation (CAPS) developed by the Missouri Association for Community Action.

CAPS is a unique tool that community action agencies use to educate everyone, from policy makers to local community leaders, about the day-to-day realities of life with a shortage of money and an abundance of stress. CAPS is a copyrighted tool made available by the Missouri Association for Community Action to organizations that want to promote a greater understanding of poverty.

During the simulation, participants role-play the lives of low-income families, from single parents trying to care for their children to senior citizens trying to maintain their self-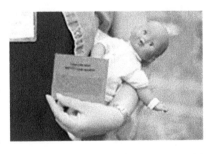sufficiency on Social Security. Imagine your fifteen-year-old daughter as the proud parent of a new baby is one of the scenarios. Your task within this family dynamic would be to provide food, shelter, and other basic necessities during the two-hour simulation while interacting with various fictitious community resources staffed by ECCO staff members.

Although it uses "play" money and other props, fictional scenarios, and time limits, we have to remind participants that

CAPS is not a game. It is a simulation tool that enables participants to view poverty from different angles in an experiential setting.

It's used as an educational tool to sensitize the community to the practical realities of a daily life constrained by limited financial resources. Participants are paired up with an ECCO team member to make up a fictitious family.

Our most interesting simulations involved local judicial members as participants. Public defenders and prosecutors came into the gym where the simulation was held. There was little conversation between the two groups until members of each group were separately assigned to the same fabricated family. As soon as the simulation started, they began to conspire and plot and plan about how they would survive. Several of the families had teenagers who were single parents, dropouts, or students who had been expelled. Many teenagers lived at home unsupervised. During the day, when family members were at work or visiting social service agencies or trying to get a job, the teens would steal from other families who weren't at home. *Now, these guys were attorneys!* One simulation had an adult who was arrested and had to go to jail. During his sentence, he escaped and literally ran out of the building. Another memorable moment was when a female worker led a strike in the factory demanding higher wages, like actress Sally Field in the movie *Norma Rae*. In all the simulations we conducted, there were instances we had never dealt with, but leave it to the judicial community to color outside the lines.

We have held multiple simulations in the past six years. More than a thousand local community educators, business leaders, law enforcement officials, health care executives, housing officials, and agency executives have participated in this educational program. Other groups who call on us to conduct it include the College of Charleston, MUSC, and Trident United Way. The Charleston Chamber of Commerce conducts the program annually as a finale to its ten-month Leadership Charleston program.

Poverty simulation with Leadership Charleston

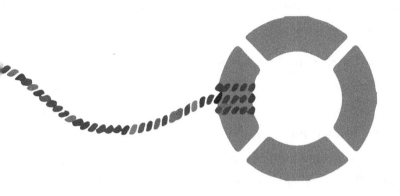

CHAPTER 4
Premise of Mission

The vision that has driven my life and career was a mission trip in 1980. I joined the singles group of First Baptist Church of Columbia, South Carolina, to minister to Philadelphia's Frankfort Avenue community. There, God gave me a vision of doing citywide ministry. We ministered to the children in this depressed area by leading arts and crafts, recreation, and Bible lessons. One afternoon I was sent to carry supplies in the church van to another ministry site across town. As I was driving, God gave me His vision; I envisioned Philadelphia and various kinds of ministry sites across the city meeting the needs of people of all ages, races, and lifestyles. To this day, this has been my "Bethel"— the point of reference for what God called me to do.

When I returned home, I couldn't get that vision off my mind. I tried ignoring it, reasoning with it, denying it. But it never went away. I began considering leaving my dad's business, where I would have no worry about future income. If I stayed there, I would be set for life.

Then I met with the minister who took us on the trip to discuss the vision; he told me he knew what I was going to say before I said it. Then I met with a former high school football coach who had left his successful career to go into the ministry. He told me the same thing, "Jack, I knew why you were coming to meet with me." After that, I began compiling a list during my devotional times about why I should stay and continue working in my dad's successful business and why I should go. Trying to be analytical, the pros and cons equaled each other. There was no evidence to support remaining where I was or leaving on a new venture. At the end of the day, it was a decision to trust and obey the Lord or not. I decided to trust what God was leading me to do.

In all three places of ministry served over the years, the vision He gave never came to fruition immediately. I didn't ask for a map or a schedule of what, when, and where things would happen in my life. But as Martin Luther King Jr. said, "You don't have to see the whole staircase. Just take the first step." That was my position then and now, in my life and in my work. I see God in action, and I choose to get involved. I don't need to see the final resting place. I have learned faith is a journey.

Every visionary leader has the promise of their God-given vision while enduring the challenges of threat and failure. Vision is the driving force behind any great work to be done. Recalling the vision is the refuge where a leader goes when things turn sour, when failure seems imminent, and when life loses its purpose. It is the safeguard when the people you lead think you're foolish, the immovable object when the sand begins sifting under your feet. It's the light in the midst of the darkness.

Through more than twenty-five years of ministry, I have learned a lot about how to do things, but the vision has always been there. The vision is not always crystal clear when it's received, but it always sets the course of direction and, along the way, situations and circumstances (or, as many say, "coincidences") take place.

These circumstances, particularly those beyond my control, guide my work. So when people ask me (as they often do), "Jack, what projects do you plan to begin in the next year?" I shrug my shoulders and answer, "I don't know." Instead, I'm always looking for opportunities to create ministry, and I never plan to accomplish a specific set of goals to begin new work.

Many years ago, I took a course centered on Henry Blackaby's Experiencing God. It really helped me understand how ministry unfolded around me. This was the normal process in seeing ministry develop, and Blackaby's study verified it. Reflecting on my years of ministry, I was able to see how my ministry journey mirrored the experience of the noted evangelical pastor; the studies helped me see the need and the possibility of creating needed ministry opportunities.

One way we find ministry opportunities is by conducting community surveys. In doing so, we may find the need for an after-school program. In previous positions, a local church would be contacted with the intention of getting members involved and raising money to support the program. If I was successful, we would move ahead with it. If unsuccessful, the program would not begin. I always saw this as God leading and directing me to open opportunities of ministry.

Experiencing God gives a sound and practical theological explanation of the way Blackaby has seen God work in his life and ministry on the mission field. Blackaby was raised in western Canada. He became a pastor and served as a consultant in North America by being employed by the Southern Baptist mission board. He has also consulted for many top corporate executives, and he led the National Prayer Day at the White House several times. Why has he been so popular? His emphasis is on an interactive relationship with God.

The first point in his explanation of how he has seen God work begins with a simple premise: God is always moving and working to accomplish His purposes of bringing the world to Him. Blackaby shows this premise throughout the Bible, especially in the life of Moses.

Knowing that God is working, believers—through having a personal relationship with Him—are aware that His mighty hand is making things happen. God moves in even the most incidental ways.

As we live our lives day by day, moment by moment, He invites us to be part of His work. When we recognize the invitation (His speaking to us), we have to decide if we will be faithful and work with Him or not. This is called a "crisis of belief."

After we accept His invitation, then we are called to adjust, which means to do our part. When we follow through, we experience an entirely new level of relationship with Him because God is always true to His word. As a result, our faith becomes stronger.

In 2015, the leader of a local rural group of residents called "Hearts of Huger," whose mission is to create a better community in Huger, told Rachel Vane, the ECCO director of volunteer engagement, about a family who had lost all they had in a house fire a couple of weeks before. The man, who was also a member of the "Hearts of Huger" organization, really needed a car.

Here's the situation as Rachel explained it:

> In March, Jerry Herman from Nucor Steel stopped by to see me about his concerns for a coworker. His coworker was the recent victim of a house fire that also destroyed his car that was parked beside his home. He asked me if we ever received donations of trailers or cars. As fate would have it, the week before one of my volunteers had come to see me and shared that he and his wife were looking for a new car and would like to donate their van once they had purchased another vehicle. I told Jerry the situation; we were both ecstatic. A week later Jerry brought his coworker to ECCO, and we gave him the title and the keys. He was speechless. As the tears ran down his cheeks, he told us that no one had ever done anything like this for him before. He said he would be able to get back and forth to work instead of walking three miles each way, as well as pick up family and friends for church.

Can you see the process Blackaby explained? God was moving; Rachel was keen on seeing His hand at work (invited to participate). She heard God speak through the volunteer. Then she had to decide if she would commit to following His invitation (crisis of belief; decided to join in) and connect the volunteer with this family in need. The adjustment was linking the two together and getting the paperwork part of the transaction completed. As a result of this, she began walking in a deeper relationship with God, knowing again that He is always at work. Her relationship was deepened as she began a truer sense of expectancy.

Almost every day we see something like this take place at ECCO. But let me caution you: Sometimes we may think God is inviting us to join in His movement when He is not. Many times I have thought He had extended invitations when He had not. Sometimes it takes a period of time to see it come to fruition after we are obedient. When he invites and speaks to me, I take it one step at a time. In other words, I don't sell the whole store at once, because I know God's timing is not always my timing. Frequently, it takes more time for the next step(s) to develop in a situation.

It's important to know that God is always moving and working to accomplish His purposes of bringing the world to Him. He also wants to include us in His redemptive work. His desire is to have a healthy relationship with all mankind. This experience has always led me in ministry.

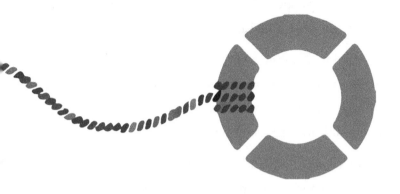

CHAPTER 5
Vision

W hat does it mean "to have vision"? I have heard many speeches and lectures on the subject and found that envisioning the future has many connotations. To some it means ignoring the past. To others it says you're out of touch. Wikipedia has several meanings, including "a supernatural experience that conveys a revelation." To me, envisioning the future is to see how life should or could be. Some consultants and writers call it the "preferred future." A purpose-driven vision sees the future with its mission fulfilled.

It could be said, "Vision is an idea followed with determined action." Or as author Anurag Prakash Ray says: "To be a success only in vision or dream is not enough. It requires hard work, courage, patience, and determination, too."

Recently I attended Stanford University's Nonprofit Management Institute and heard Barbara Bush, CEO and founder of

Global Health Corps, speak. I like her definition of vision as being "The art of seeing what is invisible to others."

After serving a summer with the Charleston Baptist Association, I saw vision of ministry sights throughout Charleston County. I could see these in the inner city, tourist areas, migrant camps, and multi-housing communities.

Ten years later, thousands of volunteers and staff were in fifty-three multi-housing communities including the inner city. We conducted sports camps in almost twenty locations, worked in fourteen tourist areas and eighteen migrant camps, rehabbed more than five hundred houses in the inner city, and established both a medical and dental clinic. Through a lot of hard work, Charleston became the top location in the country by engaging the most volunteers, according to the North American Mission Board (NAMB). In 1995, our ministry was named the national ministry location by NAMB.

When I came to ECCO in 2005, it was an unrefined gem in its service to the community. But it was a dream come true as a human service provider, since there were so many services offered to help the poor in one location. The dream of people who came looking for help and a sign of hope found it in one place and did not have to travel the county to find other assistance. This meant the ones who could not afford to put gas in their car didn't have to waste excessive fuel to get their needs met. Wasted time for appointments they faced at many other service providers was eliminated. ECCO was created and designed to give the client maximum service at the minimal expense.

Some say having the gift of being a visionary is a detriment. These are the people who always ask "how" and "why." A lot of times I see them only as critics or as trying to prevent me from doing what I know should happen. Too many times I assume these critics see what I see: a vision fully flourished and successful. But where I see an accomplished vision—volunteers involved; needs being met; people being fulfilled in one way or another, whether that be through temporary relief or by realizing their full God-given potential—critics can't seem to understand the first step. Instead, they say things like: "How are we going to pay for it?" "Why should we start something new when we have all we can handle now?" "We haven't perfected what we're doing now." "What about liability?" "Why can't the people do it for themselves?" "We don't have the staff or resources." When I hear these questions and comments, I am reminded of the great quote from the movie *Cool Hand Luke*: "What we've got here is failure to communicate." Unfortunately, this is an area I often overlook.

Fortunately, along with vision come directives that guide a visionary. Since you can't see the ultimate destination of your life, I believe God provides us with directives to lead us in the right way. He has for me. What are directives? They are the signs and opportunities along the way that bring you to the fruition of your vision; they are happenstances, such as when someone calls and says they want us to begin new programs in their community. These directives have guided me to start new ministries and to meet new people who can help financially support or volunteer in our work.

Early in 2007, I had an epiphany after being with ECCO for a little over a year. My routine each morning is to walk to the grocery store next door to buy an apple for my morning snack. This morning would be different.

When I walked out into the lobby where our clients wait to be served, I recognized many faces among the people who had come for help. This morning I saw them in a different light. I noticed how there was a sense of despair and hopelessness on each and every face in the room. Their despondency made the lobby feel very depressing. At that moment, something groundbreaking happened: the Lord spoke to me with the message, "Jack, you're really not helping these people. You're only sustaining them." I went on to the store to get my apple and began thinking about what I had heard. I asked myself, "How do we do this?"

In the fall of 2007, the answer to my epiphany was given. This would be the change of vision and mission of ECCO. It came when I attended the Sisters of Charity's (a private statewide foundation in South Carolina) tenth anniversary luncheon in Columbia. The featured speaker was Ruby Payne, an educator who had worked with inner-city children. She left her teaching career to begin addressing poverty and how it affects the people who live in it day to day, year to year, and generation to generation. In her talk, Payne contrasted how lifestyles of poverty differ from the lifestyles of the middle and upper classes. She explained why the poor purchase TVs and cars they cannot afford, why they would not leave their current and historical environments to make a better life, and other behavior I had witnessed over the years. Payne made all my experience and observations of working with the poor connect with a deeper understanding.

After buying and reading Payne's books, I was astounded how all the characteristics of the poor were capsulated into a comprehensive but simple list. I had a new understanding in spite of all my years of experience. I bought enough books for every board member. Over the next three years, ECCO hosted citywide seminars featuring a coauthor of *Bridges Out of Poverty*, one of Payne's books, and we began to implement the principles from the book into our organization. This was the beginning of our mission transformation and organizational transformation. To enrich our progress over the years, we have continued to find other ideas from around the country and incorporate them into our principles and practices. These principles are:

1. Understanding the Mental Models of Poverty, Middle Class, and Upper Class

2. Grasping the Four Causes of Poverty

3. Knowing the Hidden Rules of Poverty

4. Realizing the Voices of Language Used by Those in Poverty

This was the beginning of our antipoverty efforts in East Cooper. To my knowledge, we were the first nonprofit in the metro Charleston area that had this kind of empowerment model as our focus of purpose. This proved to be challenging because it was a new concept for human services in the tri-county area, but it was well received by our donors and led to an increase in donations. In 2011, Trident United Way began promoting and emphasizing the same theme.

This is when I realized that one of the immediate barriers that put people in poverty was the lack of education. I met occasionally with Lucy Beckham, the principal of Wando High School, to get her support and involvement. She told me that when kids drop out of school, there is no way of keeping track of them. I inquired with the Charleston County Schools about who taught the GED classes in East Cooper. I was told the high school equivalency courses were not offered anywhere in our 1,500-square-mile service area. I couldn't believe it! We immediately contracted with the school district and began offering the class at ECCO, which has been well received. This was the beginning of our Empowerment program.

Jack Little in his office at ECCO.

Today, following the Lord's directive, many other classes on a broad range of topics are offered under the Empowerment banner. These classes include: single mom support, budgeting and money management, borrowing money, job readiness, interviewing skills, resume writing, typing, social skills, and an investment match program. Class selection will continue to grow as the need is discovered. Hundreds of people have participated, and they and their families have benefited; we've seen the unemployed become employed, savings accounts opened, degrees attained, job promotions and better jobs secured, and first homes purchased.

God gives the vision of what can be. Following the directives from above will get you there, but you have to add action to the directives. All of the above resulted after following the directives that God gave along the way.

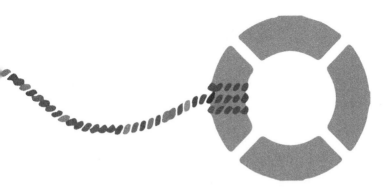

CHAPTER 6
Integrity

Integrity is the personal trait of being honest and having strong moral principles and uprightness. Integrity is the element that long-term trust and relationships are built upon. Zig Ziglar says, "Honesty and integrity are absolutely essential for success in life—all areas of life. The really good news is that anyone can develop both honesty and integrity."

Integrity is the basis on which every relationship in life is built. Bankers, businesspeople, community leaders—even some criminals—can have integrity and be successful in their endeavors by doing what they say they will do and treating others with respect.

A human services nonprofit must be constructed on integrity. Integrity is the foundation on which success is built, and telling partnering organizations/residential managers/community leaders up front about the expectations for, and plusses and minuses of, our activities is essential. When an event is good, we let partners know. But we also contact them as soon as possible if an event or an occurrence goes wrong because we know a manager has enough headaches and worries without some outside organization causing problems.

During my first Christmas at ECCO, our doors were opened for service the week following the holiday for the first time in the organization's history. Prior to my arrival, no services were provided. The board urged me to change this policy because its members realized that people may encounter a food crisis during that time. I decided to have a skeletal staff work a half-day schedule that week to be present and available to help these needs.

One day as I was sitting in my office, a man I had never met, Danny Rowland, came in and asked if I could help him. He said that during their last Christmas celebration, his wife and three grown daughters had their traditional celebration where they gathered around the Christmas tree and opened presents. They ripped off all the wrappings and showed their gifts to each other. He explained, "They just sat there looking at each other and feeling empty." He pointed out that his family had all they needed. So he wanted that year's Christmas to be something different, something special. He told me he wanted to give a donation to ECCO in the name of each daughter and asked me to write a letter to each one that would be presented to them as their Christmas present. The letter would describe how the money would help different people in different ways. I agreed to the idea, and he wrote the check. I had never met this man; I had no clue who he was. So I could have gone about my own agenda for the day, but I didn't. I told the man I would write the letters, so I did.

Danny came by the next day to pick up the letters. It was an opportune time to tell him how we were very conservative about how our funding limited administrative costs. I explained that only 7 percent of our revenue went to overhead costs, while 93 percent went directly to client services. Danny liked that. He already knew that all the money stayed local.

The next week, I received a call from Danny. He was elated. "It was the best Christmas we have ever had, Jack!" he told me. "When it came time for my daughters to get their presents, I gave them the envelope and asked them to read your letter." He said, "Each one cried when they finished reading it. We truly celebrated the blessing, the true meaning of Christmas this year!" I did what I said I would do, and it paid off for Danny's family and more. It is still paying off today.

I didn't hear from Danny again until the following Christmas. He told me he was one of three owners of the local shipyard. Each Christmas, he said, the owners would give to almost any charity that called. But this year they wanted to be wiser about it. He explained that they had grown tired of giving to groups where the money goes off to a national organization while the local community sees very little of it, if any. They had also grown tired of learning that some charities had such high administrative costs that very little would be given to the cause.

He told me the owners had come to an agreement about their future donations. They would divide their profit equally each year and could pick their own local charity to support. One chose the local free medical clinic at the shipyard. Another chose the local food bank. Danny chose ECCO because he trusted me and I had fulfilled his request the year before.

The story doesn't stop there. Three years ago, I asked Danny to consider being on our board of directors. He immediately agreed. In the board interview and at his first board meeting, he told the story of the three letters and how I did what I said I would do. He continues to tell the story every time he meets with a group to talk about how he got involved with us. That's what I call payoff! Danny now serves as chairman of our development and fund-raising committee. In 2014 Danny led the committee in raising over $490,000!

So integrity is about being true to your word. Relationships are built on trust. Trust is earned through integrity. Integrity is doing what you say you will do, no matter the ultimate cost.

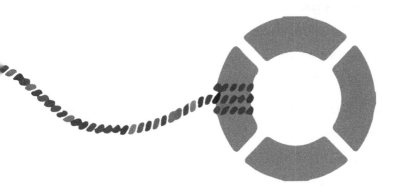

CHAPTER 7
Why We Are All
Called to Help

Helping the poor? Some people argue, "They should help themselves. I was poor once, and I overcame it. If they would just get a job, they wouldn't need welfare." Many see the poor as being conniving, lazy, unintelligent, or even parasitic.

Today, blame may fall to the individual or the parents. Drug and alcohol problems are common reasons for people being poor. Another is unwed moms with irresponsible baby daddies. The lack of morals and/or ethics that have been passed down through generations is a valid cause. Many other people argue that their situation is the government's fault.

My stance is that the individual is in their situation due to numerous causes. But in America, in addition to human nature, there has to be a specific cause for such a dilemma. If research were conducted to address the problem of poverty today and through-out history, the report would come back with a list of "top three causes" and how they could be addressed. Blame has to be placed on someone or something; that's just how America operates.

This chapter is not an apologetic justification of why the poor are with us. There are many reasons that could be used to explain their situations. Many of those on government assistance need to get their lives in order and become self-sufficient. But believe it or not, we have families where both parents work and don't make a combined income above the poverty level—one reason why we should be considerate of those who lack the basic resources of life.

Poverty is a situation where usually no one is to blame. It is the result of the way an individual is born into the world. We have no control over where we begin in life. South Carolina's Governor Nikki Haley has told her story of being raised in a small South Carolina town in the 1970s.[10] Her parents were immigrants from India, and she never felt she fit in. She wasn't white or black, and all the kids told her so. She was picked on because of her "brown" skin color. The white children would tell her, "You're not white." The black children would tell her, "You're not black." Haley said, "You can't change how you were born. You can't change who you're born from. Every person should be proud no matter who your parents are and where they've come from." During her tenure, Haley has overcome tremendous obstacles as a minority—a woman of Indian ancestry serving in a southern state—and in leading our state through an extremely difficult time with the

---

10 Jennifer Berry Hawes, "Grieving Gov. Nikki Haley forever changed by church massacre," The Post and Courier, July 18, 2015, accessed September 6, 2015, http://www.postandcourier.com/article/20150718/PC1603/150719396/1031/grieving-gov-nikki-haley-forever-changed-by-church-massacre.

Mother Emanuel church shootings that shined a spotlight on the racial divide and the removal of the Confederate flag from our statehouse grounds.

But not everyone rises to the top rung of the ladder as Haley has. When I worked in Gainesville, Georgia, Gene Beckstein, a retired schoolteacher who was a very caring and compassionate layman, began a feeding program in a government housing community. He provided lunch for hundreds of people each week. He delivered powerful messages when he spoke publicly about his ministry. He would ask, "When you were born, who chose to be born with brown hair? Who chose to have brown eyes? Who asked to be born into a white family? Who asked to be born into a middle class family? Raise your hand." Gene's point was that none of us had made prior arrangements to be in the lives we were born into. We had no control of where we landed on earth.

Think about it. If your grandmother was black and was denied a home loan or employment in the 1950s, that influenced where your parents grew up, which then affected where you grew up. Where you live determines where you go to school, and since the community's tax dollars support local schools, it's easy to see why poor neighborhoods end up with poorly funded schools. Your opportunity was limited because the resources were.

So why should we help the poor? First is the opportunity to improve our world by taking care of our fellow man. Second is the personal fulfillment we receive. And third is the blessing of being faithful to God's call to serve Him by serving others.

Pope Francis said, "Poverty for us Christians is not a sociological, philosophical, or cultural category, no. It is theological ... because our God, the Son of God ... made Himself poor to walk along the road with us."[11] The Pope, a student of the teachings of Ignatius, leads us to be incarnational—that is, we leaders especially are to imitate Jesus, someone who willingly plunged into a messy world and nonetheless remained undeterred from His vision of how human beings ought to treat one another.

Our fellow man is to be treated with dignity and respect. We learn to take on the humble nature of a servant. Every day I pray for Jesus to use me as His hands and His feet. This is when I feel the most like Christ. I am overwhelmed realizing I am reflecting Jesus in the flesh.

So why should we help our neighbor who is struggling financially? The first reason is we have the opportunity to change another person's life for the better. Making a change for the betterment of the world is what most people want.

When our children learn to walk, we become ecstatic with their accomplishment. We call our family, take pictures, and mark down the date. As my children grew up, we charted their growth by marking a line on the wall of their height and putting a date beside it. Every few months, we would do it again. Over time, you could see how much each had grown; this was such a fun and meaningful experience for the whole family.

Instead of serving the poor as being a burden, I see serving them as an opportunity. In Matthew 25, the disciples asked Jesus, "When did we see you hungry or thirsty or a stranger or needing clothes or sick or in prison?" Jesus replied, "Truly I tell you,

---

11 Pope Francis, "Address of the Holy Father Francis," May 18, 2013, video, Saint Peter's Square, The Holy See website, accessed September 6, 2015, https://w2.vatican.va/content/francesco/en/speeches/2013/may/documents/papa-francesco_20130518_veglia-pentecoste.html

whatever you did for one of the least of these brothers and sisters of mine, you did for me."

It's so inspiring to assist someone pursuing the pathway to discover their full potential. Helping people rise above their situations and enabling them to live full lives where they're contributing to society makes an impact on the world. Teaching someone to balance their budget, pay off debt, and become employable is an exciting adventure to share. And it's extremely satisfying to help a client open his first bank account and begin saving money, then seeing his savings matched three times over and the money used to continue his education, buy the family's first home, or start a business. We see these situations play out at ECCO frequently. Then we hold parties and celebrate what these clients have achieved. It's like seeing your own child taking its first step.

Helping others is our moral obligation. When I was in high school, the University of California, Los Angeles (UCLA) had its record-setting winning streak come to an end at the hands of Notre Dame. Then-coach John Wooden had led UCLA to yet-to-be-topped eighty-eight consecutive wins. Wooden knew how to motivate his players to do the right things, to excel, and to be the best. His knowledge and wisdom spread beyond basketball.

The oft-quoted leader once said: "Be true to yourself, help others, make each day your masterpiece, make friendship a fine art, drink deeply from good books—especially the Bible, build a shelter against a rainy day, give thanks for your blessings, and pray for guidance every day." He taught that success is derived from projecting your life and its successes to help impact and change the lives of others through everyday enrichment and living.

In a perfect America, anyone can climb the ladder to success: work hard and overcome barriers—anyone can do this if they have the fortitude and determination. No one gets laid off or fired. Everyone has health insurance and a 401k. Bankruptcy is not possible, and every child goes to private school and then on to college. Everyone has a successful career that will carry them to a very comfortable retirement. The American Dream can be a wonderful journey for many, but there are others who cannot even fantasize about it.

When we become motivated by a self-consumed society, we become silos consumed with self-absorption. Friendships are few. And we become consumed with what positions we can obtain and what treasures and toys we can buy to make ourselves feel competitive in the race with our neighbors. But pursuit of worldly material possessions gives life a hollow purpose. Soon, the toys and possessions entrap us in an endless race with empty meaning. Frustration builds as we finally discover we can't have it all.

St. Ignatius of Loyola said we pursue our money, power, or honor, but once we grasp them, they end up controlling us. He called this pursuit "the enemy of human nature." The world teaches today that personal success is the "be all and end all of life." People are consumed with appointments, meetings, and making quotas. When goals are reached, personal emptiness is inevitable. Over time, the undertow of personal satisfaction becomes hard to resist. Bonuses seem generous until we find out our partner received twice as much. Ignatius called this "vain honor from the world, and finally to surging pride."[12] Our world begins to revolve

---

12 Lowney, Chris. 2013. Pope Francis: Why He Leads the Way He Leads. Chicago: Loyola Press.

around ourselves, what we earn, and what others think about us. Life's most important things are lost. Family takes a back burner. Life's most precious possessions are lost. Life is meant to be much more than this. It's essential we discover deeper meanings for life.

The second reason for us to help the less fortunate is for personal satisfaction. People like to help because it makes them feel good about themselves. At face value this is the most selfish reason of all to help someone else; personal fulfillment is a byproduct of helping someone. Through my almost thirty years of ministry and engaging volunteers, the most common remark I hear is, "They benefited me more than I benefited them. It was such a rewarding experience."

As a boy, whenever Stephen Post, professor of preventive medicine at Stony Brook University School of Medicine, got a bad grade, or felt left out of the games his older brother and sister were playing, or was otherwise having a rough day, his mother always said, "Why don't you go out and do something for someone else?" At which point he'd head next door to rake his neighbor's leaves or go across the street to help another neighbor with his boat. "I always came home feeling better," Post said. It turns out there was science behind his mom's kitchen-table wisdom.[13]

Serving others makes an incomparable impact on our personal lives. We have a longer lifespan, and we are happier.

---

13 Leslie Goldman, "4 Amazing Health Benefits of Helping Others," Huffington Post, December 28, 2013, accessed September 6, 2015, http://www.huffingtonpost.com/2013/12/28/health-benefits-of-helping-others_n_4427697.html.

Studies have found that serving the poor can add years to your life—with some evidence pointing to a 22 percent reduction in mortality. How much time does it take? A separate study found that seniors who gave one hundred hours or more annually were 28 percent less likely to die from any cause than their less-philanthropic peers. "But that's not a magic number—it could be 75 hours or 125," says study coauthor Elizabeth Lightfoot, Ph.D., an associate professor at the University of Minnesota School of Social Work. "The important thing is that you're doing it regularly." And you needn't be older to benefit. A new study in JAMA Pediatrics found that high school students saw a drop in their cholesterol levels after volunteering with younger kids once a week for two months.[14]

There are health benefits as well:

A 2013 study in the journal *Psychology and Aging* revealed that adults over the age of fifty who reported volunteering at least two hundred hours in the past year (roughly four hours per week) were 40 percent less likely than non-volunteers to have developed hypertension four years later. Though researchers don't fully understand why giving back can have such a marked impact on blood pressure, they believe it may be linked to the stress-reducing effects of being both active and altruistic. "As we get older, our social networks shrink," says study coauthor Rodlescia Sneed.[15]

14 Ibid.

15 Ibid.

Serving others offers "an opportunity to establish more social connections and form new bonds with people who care about you and motivate you to take care of yourself."[16]

When you read to the elderly, walk a 5K for cancer, or even plunk a quarter in the Salvation Army kettle, the reward center of your brain pumps out the mood-elevating neurotransmitter dopamine, creating what researchers call a helper's high. In fact, one study found that people who completed five small acts of kindness (like helping a friend, visiting a relative, or writing a thank-you note) one day a week for six weeks experienced a significant boost in overall feelings of well-being.[17]

The third and most compelling reason to help another is Biblically based. The Bible inspires believers to be like God, as we are created in his image to be like Him. When we conform to His image of giving rather than getting, we receive God's blessings.

This dates back to the Old Testament, which describes followers presenting sacrifices to make amends for their selfishness. This, they thought, was adequate, but it was not. Isaiah 1:11 says, "'What makes you think I want all your sacrifices?' says the Lord. 'I am sick of your burnt offerings of rams and the fat of fattened cattle. I get no pleasure from the blood of bulls and lambs and goats.'" The Old Testament basically ends with man never mending or repairing the broken relationship and separation from God.

The Bible talks about how the poor and afflicted, the widows, and the orphaned are to receive our mercy as He has demonstrated

---

16 Ibid.

17 Ibid.

in our lives. We, in essence, become His hands as we touch the less fortunate.

Being responsible by caring for the poor plays a big role in the Scriptures.

Throughout the Old Testament, the Israelites were instructed to help the poor. We have to remember that Jesus lived among the poor. He chose to live with them, eat with them, and confide in them. Jesus came to the world as one. He was born in a feeding trough. When circumcised, his parents presented two pigeons as their offering—which was prescribed for the poorest class of people in society.

On his final trip to Jerusalem, Jesus rode on a borrowed donkey, spent the evening in a borrowed room, and was laid in a borrowed tomb. His possessions were claimed by the role of dice. He died naked and penniless. He had little the world valued, and the little he had was taken. He was discarded, but only because of Him do we have any hope.[18]

Helping the poor can be a spiritual breakthrough for many. Many devout Christians have predetermined notions that their faith is completed by living righteously, obeying the Ten Commandments, being baptized, attending church, evangelizing, and giving money. The plight of the poor is ignored, as the focus is solely on saving souls rather than poverty and social conditions. Priority of

18 Keller, Timothy. 2010. Generous Justice. New York: Riverhead Books.

the real practice of Christianity is given to sharing the good news about Jesus and His death and resurrection. Although important, I don't believe these are the only facts to base Christianity on. The area of compassion and kindness to the widow, orphans, and the poor fulfills the teachings of Christ and cannot be disregarded.

James, chapters 14–18, says it best:

> "What good is it, my brothers, if someone says he has faith but does not have works? Can that faith save him? If a brother or sister is poorly clothed and lacking in daily food and one of you says to them, 'Go in peace, be warmed, and filled,' without giving them the things needed for the body, what good is that? So also faith by itself, if it does not have works, is dead.
>
> "But someone will say, 'You have faith and I have works.' Show me your faith apart from your works, and I will show you my faith by my works."

Helping the poor and the working poor is the greatest opportunity to serve others, ourselves, and the Lord. Volunteering is the greatest chance to fulfill our lives. The personal benefits truly outweigh the costs as we have seen. God's promises of blessing those who serve the poor will never fade away.

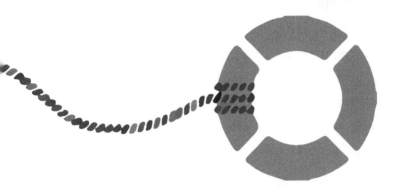

CHAPTER 8
Raising Money

I grew up in sales. I sold cleaning services for my dad's business and sold life insurance for a period of time before coming to ECCO. You get really thick-skinned when trying to sell life insurance. Personally, I don't mind asking for money. I see the money as helping clients, not me. If I were asking for money for my own personal needs, I wouldn't be able to do it.

As this chapter begins, let me clarify that ECCO receives no government funding and has no desire to receive it. I am proud of the fact that we are totally supported by the local community and private foundations. ECCO's support is a model of how the community can and should come together to fund and support services for the poor and working poor.

When I came to ECCO in 2005, revenues had fallen short of the annual goal. The budget was the main concern of the board and the reason for finding a new director. That year, revenue was less than $300,000, and ECCO had seen years of falling short of their budget goals. Today, revenue is at $1.5 million. Something I learned a long time ago working with my dad was to listen and learn. By doing this, I could find answers to questions such as: How does someone excel at their business? What other methods do they use to accomplish the same job? How can they do it better? How can they perform the same job more efficiently?

But I was naïve and ignorant about what it meant to really raise money. My experience was limited to the support of local Baptist churches. Fund-raising in denominational life is very different than in an independent nonprofit. In denominational life, fund-raising is totally dependent on contributions by members. These limited sources of income are all churches have to rely on to maintain their ministries and operations.

Still, when I worked with the Baptist churches, I was able to raise large sums of money and establish continued streams of revenue for Bonnie Doone, the conference center of the Charleston Baptist Association, and for Charleston Outreach, the mission program of the association.

But the opportunity at ECCO was completely different. It was imperative for me to learn about approaching potential donors who had limited knowledge and no affiliation with the nonprofit. I knew, as in previous positions, that people must become familiar with a need or a goal before they will entertain the idea of being involved or giving financial support. Grant writing and filing related reports were also new territory.

Publicity for ECCO became a major priority. In addition to telling our story, I believed a special event or a fund-raiser was the way to increase income and support for our mission. I even imagined a membership program that would enlist supporters for $25 per year. The program would put stickers on everyone's car, and ECCO would become a household name. If we enlisted one thousand people, that would create an annual revenue stream of $25,000. Little did I know the discipline of conducting an aggressive fund-raising campaign would teach me the basics of obtaining financial support.

ADVANCING THE MISSION CAMPAIGN

The second financial campaign, "Advancing the Mission," began in 2005. $1.3 million was raised for building renovations, disaster relief, and basic operations allowed ECCO to begin catalyzing community grassroots disaster preparedness strategy and involvement of the community in defining future initiatives. The funds led to space renovation, which allowed inclusion of the Catholic Charity Immigration Center. Later, unused space was configured in partnership with the Medical University of South Carolina into a medical office to house a family medicine practice and a free emergency medical clinic (C.A.R.E. Clinic). Further refinements to the 2003 building allowed space for private counseling rooms, teaching classrooms, and computer-based education classrooms. Most recently, ECCO started the Partners in HealthCare clinic with the MUSC College of Nursing. ECCO clients are seen in that clinic by nurse practitioners through referral and by appointment from ECCO. The physical changes to the 2003 "new facility" reflect the overall strategic plan to meet the ongoing needs of the communities east of the Cooper River (Del Bene and Galasso).

The concept of raising money through a capital campaign is very simple and straightforward if you are in a bricks and mortar project. Buildings are tangible. They can be touched, and beautiful drawings of them inspire the public with images of what could be.

The campaign initiated in 2004, called "Advancing the Mission" (ATM), was different. The major reason for having the campaign was to generate operating expenses for the next five years, with a goal of $1.2 million. The effort had a slow beginning and was lifeless when I arrived. The campaign waned as prospect lists were exhausted. We all recognized that we needed a professional to help us accomplish the campaign.

After we had interviewed several professional fund-raisers, out of the blue, a man came into my office that had been in fund-raising at Georgetown University. His name was Clark Thompson. He had recently moved to Mount Pleasant and was seeking an organization to work part time with. He had previously been executive director for the YMCA in inner-city Baltimore and regional director for the organization in Washington, D.C., which assured me he knew what it was like to serve the poor and working poor. Plus, he knew how to raise big money. His words convinced me that one "ask" (the verbal request for a donation) of $5,000 or even $25,000 was more feasible and much less taxing than raising small amounts from the multitudes.

After he had asked me some very direct, hard, and even intimidating questions, I made an appointment to introduce him to our chairman, Pat Ilderton, who raised the bulk of the campaign funds on his own. We decided Clark's fees were nominal, especially after interviewing other fund-raisers. Pat and I realized his experience and that we could get him at a bargain, and we agreed to hire him as a consultant.

Benefit Focus held a winter coat drive for ECCO.

Clark became my personal advisor and publicist. Early on, we went to a major grand opening of the headquarters of Benefitfocus, a new computer software company on Daniel Island. I had met the founder and CEO, Shawn Jenkins, just a couple of months before, and I was so pleased he invited me.

At the grand opening, the president of the state's largest insurance company was there. This company had been a huge investor in Benefitfocus. Clark introduced me to him as the executive director of East Cooper Community Outreach, and the insurance executive seemed to be impressed with that. From that time on, I knew we had made the right hiring decision.

The challenge of accomplishing the ATM goal lay before us. We had to come up with an appealing strategy for supporters to buy into. The strategy was to divide the effort into several areas where our work would be appealing and relatable to the general public. The campaign, we decided, would generate support for three areas of our work. First was for ongoing services and programs, second was for disaster preparedness, and third was for building renovation.

It was determined that 50 percent would go to ongoing services and programs. We had received some generous grants to underwrite the staff positions of client services, volunteer coordinator, and prescription assistance. When these grants expired, the ATM funding would help replace that income.

Disaster preparedness for hurricanes and other catastrophic events would claim 30 percent. This made sense in light of ECCO's origins in the aftermath of Hurricane Hugo. Starting in 2006, we began sponsoring hurricane awareness seminars for East Cooper, something no other nonprofit was doing and a unique approach that demonstrated we were preparing for the next disaster. We hired a part-time coordinator to prepare churches and other grass-roots organizations. This has been received extremely well and provided great publicity to ECCO. Since 2011, we have partnered with a local TV station for these hurricane preparedness seminars.

Each year we cosponsor the event, using the on-air time with their weatherman to invite people to come. We have also appeared on many radio and television talk shows.

We got into hurricane preparedness through an arrangement with the town of Mount Pleasant, in which the town would take control of our building as a distribution center when the next disaster stuck in exchange for waiving permit fees for our new building.

In my first board meeting, I was assigned to have the town of Mt. Pleasant install a switch for the generator to connect to our building before the next hurricane. I met with the town officials, and they explained their side of the agreement and the recovery plan after the next disaster. The emergency distribution plan assumed the churches would come and pick up supplies and take them back to their community to share with their neighbors. I asked if the churches knew about the plan, and the town's officials looked stunned. They hadn't thought of that! Thus began our first annual church disaster preparation seminar.

The other 20 percent of the ATM funds would be used for capital improvements. Staff was added as programs grew, but then a space problem began to occur. We added a computer lab, a meeting room, two offices, and four rooms for counseling; we expanded the office area in the dental clinic; and we added stairs to the attic to give needed storage space.

The campaign was divided into two phases: the silent phase and the public phase. The silent phase took three years to complete. The public phase lasted about two months.

SILENT PHASE

Our next step was training the committee of board members. Then the silent phase began. The silent phase is more strategic than the public phase, in that it is a much more intensive time and requires more effort from the staff. The board began meeting regularly to discuss names of prospective donors and how to solicit them. We pored over names and turned up stones looking for people who had a history with ECCO and had the financial capacity to help.

We made who's who lists of the community's prosperous residents and vetted them through board members and even other supporters. Appointments were set up to meet with each prospective donor while a board member was present.

Invitations were extended by the board member to the potential donor to come for the "Tour of Hope," the title for our facility tour. It's pretty much a fact in nonprofit organizations that most board members are not comfortable asking for money, but research had already determined each prospect's ability to contribute. When a potential donor expressed interest in our work, we would ask the interested donor to make an appointment to come in for a tour as a way to introduce everyone. Once the facility was toured and introductions made, Clark or myself would then be prepared to ask for a donation.

PUBLIC PHASE

Once 80 percent of the goal was raised, the public phase of the campaign was initiated. This was done by enlisting six team captains to become our advocates. Their responsibilities were to recruit at least six others to talk with their contacts and get a donation. They held social gatherings in their homes or at ECCO.

We met weekly to support, celebrate, and encourage the captains. This is a rapidly moving phase that only took about two months.

In 2008, we not only met our goal but exceeded it. The total amount raised was a little over $1.3 million. To date, I am happy to say we have used little of the 50 percent for supporting our existing programs and services.

INDIVIDUAL DONORS

We divide individual donors into two areas: individuals and businesses. Building relationships with both of these types of donors is an ongoing effort. Relationships have to be built over a period of time. As always, we invite potential donors to come by for our tour. Afterwards, we would ask which area of our programs impressed them the most, and then we look for ways to get them involved in that area. Research is done by our director of development and marketing to find helpful information on the prospect. After the prospect is involved for a few weeks, I approach and ask them if they would consider giving a certain amount.

A high percentage of our efforts are used to maintain existing donors. When these donors become ECCO supporters and feel included and kept up to date, they are likely to continue giving year after year. That's much easier than finding new donors.

In 2013, the Life Ring Society was created. This is a donor category for those who give $1,000 or more each year. They are privy to special updates and emails from the ECCO executive director. We also try to continue connecting with them in many other ways, such as through quarterly newsletters and quarterly receptions where wine and cheese are served.

I also keep a list of our thirty top donors. I review it periodically and make contact with donors if I haven't seen them recently. I call, send an email, or even set an appointment for lunch or coffee.

The key words to "making an ask" are "Would you consider...?" The word "consider" makes it easier on both the potential donor and the one asking for the donation—it is a non-threatening word and disarms the person being asked to donate. As said earlier, most board members and people in general don't like to ask for money. As they are trained, emphasis is given to using "consider."

GRANTS

Grants are a great source of income to start a new program. The danger of using grants is that they go away. They can be multiyear or annual, and although the multiyear is preferred, we are happy to receive them for a year's duration. The philosophy of using grants is to begin the designated program and then raise support through individual donations and/or fund-raisers.

Each staff director is required to watch out for grants that may apply to their programs. Currently, around 25 percent of our support is derived from grants. We have had as much as 33 percent in previous years. As a general rule of thumb, I am comfortable with around 30 percent.

FUND-RAISERS AND SPECIAL EVENTS

ECCO has a number of special events and fund-raisers each year. These kinds of events take a lot of energy from staff and volunteers, but on the plus side, they give ECCO exposure and raise money for the organization, while giving volunteers a chance to make new friends.

Our golf tournament began back in the late 1990s, but our director of development and marketing has taken it to a new level, evolving it into an event where important business deals are made. It has become one of the most popular tournaments in Charleston. In 2014, 164 participants filled two courses at the exclusive Daniel Island Club.

Until 2007, ECCO had never had a gala. Now we vary the theme every three years to keep it fresh and exciting. The first gala was the "Stone Soup Supper," a formal dinner where an inspirational speaker spoke about their journey and how it related to our mission.

The Stone Soup theme was based on a story from World War II about a soldier who came to a small European village and talked the residents into contributing what they had to make soup to feed the entire village. The highlight of the gala was the Stone Soup Award, given to the person who had contributed the most to the mission of ECCO through the years. The award continues to be given at every gala since.

In 2009 we celebrated our twentieth anniversary, and the theme of the event was "Hurricane Party." This was a huge change from the previous formal dinner; instead of suits and ties, the dress was come as you are! Dress was Bermuda shorts and T-shirts, as you would wear to a local neighborhood get-together when an oncoming storm warning was issued. The venue was decorated creatively with caution tape, Styrofoam coolers, and lanterns at each table. Local weatherman and author Bill Walsh forecasted the weather live on Live5News, a beach band played, a silent auction was held, and food was served at various stations around the event.

Joyce Darby and Marjorie Cannon at ECCO's 20th Anniversary Hurricane Party.

The "Golf Ball" has been the theme since 2013, combining the golf tournament and the gala in the same week. Mostly men play in the tournament, while their wives look forward to the gala. The golf tournament is the same format as most. The gala includes a band, live and silent auctions, and food stations. In 2015, over $200,000 was raised.

When fund-raising is mentioned among nonprofit leaders, everyone's ears perk up. Why? Because there are no magic solutions. It takes time to develop as many sources of income as ECCO has. If I were asked, "What is the most important aspect of fund-raising?" I would say relationships. Trust builds relationships, and relationships build trust.

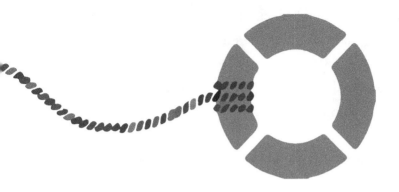

CHAPTER 9
Volunteers

A nother reason a nonprofit can provide services to the poor is involving volunteers. Our professional staff is undergirded by our more than four hundred dedicated volunteers. The services they provide keeps a nonprofit's administrative costs minimal. Not having the fixed expenses of salaries and benefits of multiple staff members up front is a major factor of separating nonprofits from expensive government agencies. Capturing the passion of the volunteers strengthens the work of a nonprofit, whereas government employees become jaded to the endless plethora of needs.

EARLY YEARS OF ECCO

"One measure of the effectiveness of the early years of ECCO may be gleaned from the Summary Activity Reports. From August through December 1990, ECCO served five hundred clients. In 1991, it served 1,753 clients. In 1990, 1,334 volunteer hours were recorded, the next year, 3,101 hours, plus 168 hours from dentists who volunteered at the free ECCO Dental Clinic" (Del Bene and Galasso).

Monetary Value of our Volunteers: $629,870

We constantly remind our volunteers that they are the most important asset ECCO has. In 2013–2014, we had volunteers give 21,163 hours, with a monetary impact of $629,870. We use fair market value for each professional service that requires a license and AARP guidelines for the general "unskilled" volunteer positions. As you would expect, dentists top the rate chart at $100 per hour, while those who serve in the warehouse are valued at $12 per hour.

Volunteers are the most valuable asset an organization can have. Working with thousands of volunteers for almost thirty years, I have seen how they can bring a vision to fruition.

My volunteer career began when I went to New York City as a senior in high school as part of a church mission group. The group was divided into three teams to serve in three of the city's five boroughs. After coming home, I realized it was the most rewarding thing I had ever done. Of course, I was mesmerized by the city and its big buildings and subway system, but reaching out and meeting people of different backgrounds and cultures was so much more fascinating. Two years later, I returned and was intrigued once again.

Seven years after the trip to New York City, when serving in Gainesville, Georgia, and after beginning several new churches in suburbia and multifamily housing communities, I realized my individual efforts would only stretch so far. Volunteers were enlisted. For example, Frances Reed directed our food pantry, "The Good Samaritan," and Ron Armister helped with our local prison ministry. I could see all of our works progressing if only we had more volunteers, but I also knew the number of local volunteers available was very limited. I reflected on my early years as a member of a church mission team in New York. We performed mission Vacation Bible School and choir performances in each of the three boroughs we served in, and I could see this effort being duplicated in Gainesville to help spread our program.

That was around 1991, about the time I was contacted to transfer to Charleston. After my family and I relocated to Charleston, I saw the same type of opportunity I had participated in as a high schooler. I envisioned how mission teams could come and work in different multi-housing communities and tourist attractions.

Having this vision, I began building relationships and working with pastors and community leaders. I also knew the importance of enlisting our local churches to sponsor these ministries and empower their members to carry the work into the future. I needed to gain trust and respect for our efforts. As a result, in 2000, we were doing ministry and programming with more than six thousand volunteers in hundreds of locations in Charleston—the largest program in the country.

TRAINING VOLUNTEERS TO ASSIST THE MISSION

It is important to know that the three key elements in working with volunteers are recruiting, training, and maintaining. Although these sound simple, it's necessary to spend time on each area to have a robust and meaningful volunteer program.

RECRUITING

My sisters called me Tom Sawyer in my younger years because I could get my friends to help me with my yard duties.

Each week, my dad assigned me the responsibility of maintaining the yard. Our yard was populated by scores of pine trees. These long-leaf, needled pines would shed their needles almost year-round, it seemed. On top of that, our grass was the very finicky zoysia. I had to use a special reel-type mower to cut it. The mower would not work if the yard had any pine needles, leaves, or other debris, so I had to rake the yard year-round. My father would not let me play until I had finished all my chores. This became problematic for my friends and me because our front yard was the neighborhood football field. These friends would come over and ask me when I would be finished. So to hurry the assignment, I told them if they helped, I would finish sooner and we could resume our football game from the day before.

My dad came home early from work one afternoon and couldn't believe his eyes. I had a yard full of my friends raking, picking up pine straw, and pulling weeds out of the shrubs. He said I was standing there giving them directions while they worked! Actually, it was a common scene in our yard. Little did I know that those days provided the groundwork in my ability to recruit volunteers.

Today, recruiting volunteers face-to-face is second nature to me, which has a lot to do with those early years. I learned that when people see something they want, they become willing to pitch in to achieve their needs and their desires. When volunteers take our "Tour of Hope" today, they see the dental and medical clinics; the classrooms; the computer lab; and the warehouse full of food, clothing, and furniture, and then it's fairly easy to get them involved. Some volunteers say today, "Jack asked me to help with a project, and now he's got me on three more!"

Volunteers must be assigned tasks that are meaningful to them and understand how their work fits into our overall mission. In our volunteer orientation, we present information about ECCO and the population we serve. We describe the various volunteer opportunities and how they fit into the everyday operations and our mission. Then we give volunteers a tour of ECCO so that they can see how the ministries fit and work together.

We also take a gifts-and-talent inventory of each volunteer and try to place them in a position where these skills are used. One volunteer, who was in computer software sales, created a system for client interviewing and volunteer management that continues to be used today. Another volunteer, an entrepreneur, is working with our clients to help them start businesses. Some volunteers with experience working as social service employees assist with client intake.

Some volunteers don't want to use their previous experiences. Case in point, recently a retired radiologist wanted to volunteer. I told her about our positions in client interviewing and the medical clinic. She let me know quickly, "I've done that all my life. I want to do something different!" We found that her interest was in working with the clients to teach basic computer skills. Another volunteer had been a judge in another state and now assists clients every Thursday afternoon in our clothing store.

Bev Genez and Leola Simmons

This brings up a very important difference between nonprofits and government agencies: passion. Organizations are chosen by volunteers because of the passion of the volunteer and the purpose of the organization. If a volunteer's interest is in the arts, they choose to be involved with an art organization. If it is with animals, they look to the humane society. If it's music—the symphony. If its drama, they look to local town theatre. ECCO involves those who care about people who struggle with poverty. Their passion is to serve this group in order that they may overcome the obstacles that keep them from becoming financially independent.

Recently a new member of the Daniel Island Rotary Club came in for the "Tour of Hope." After we finished we went into my office and asked my customary question, "What impressed you the most?" He responded by saying, "The spirit of your staff and volunteers! I've noticed in government agencies nobody wants to be there—employees or clients." Capturing the passion of the volunteers strengthens the work of a nonprofit, whereas government employees become jaded to the endless plethora of needs.

PUBLIC SPEAKING

Speaking opportunities provide a consistent flow of volunteers. Telling stories about how ECCO's programs have affected people's lives compels others to think how they could make a difference, too. I have spoken in front of hundreds of civic, church, and community groups over the years. Not everyone in attendance is interested in what I'm saying, but without a doubt, there are a few who are in every gathering.

ADS AND NEWSLETTERS

Through the years, the bulk of volunteers have been derived through ads submitted to church newsletters, in which small blurbs promoted the need for laypeople to serve in ways they may not have considered, listing the need, the hours, and who to contact.

WORD OF MOUTH

As with any advertising, the least expensive and most effective form is happy and fulfilled volunteers. Many times volunteers would tell me they had a friend who might be interested in helping out. In writing this, I realize we need to let the volunteers know it's permissible to tell their friends and even to bring them along for their next shift.

TRAINING VOLUNTEERS

On my first mission trip to New York, the most important lesson I learned about training volunteers was to give enough background information about the setting and the people who lived there. For example, classes were held to teach about New York and what situations we might find ourselves in. Training also familiarized us with the schedule of each day, the materials we would use, and the activities we would conduct.

The intensity of training volunteers varies from organization to organization. For example, hospice training is very intense because volunteers must prepare individuals and their families for death; they require hours of initial training and ongoing training. On the other hand, food banks teach volunteers how to unpack boxes of food and stack the cans on the shelves. This can be done in a couple of hours.

Volunteers must know three things about their position: the responsibilities of the position they are to fill, the time commitment the role will take, and how their role contributes to the purpose and mission of the organization.

Training long-term volunteers is a lengthy and involved process. At Charleston Outreach of the Charleston Baptist Association, we had as many as sixty-four college student volunteers each summer. Preparing them for a ten-week stint was a weeklong process. We began with an orientation of the association, its mission and purpose, policies, and rules. This was followed by the Myers-Briggs personality test, which would help the volunteers understand themselves. Since the students worked in ministry teams, team building was necessary. The programs varied widely and involved work with children, houses repairs, migrant camps, drama and choral performances in public places, sports ministries, and many other types of ministry. These diverse ministries called for specialized training in each. While this type of training may seem very complex, it has proved to be worth the effort.

RESPONSIBILITIES

Normally a new volunteer is unfamiliar with the "what" and "how to" of their role, but on-the-job training is a practice we have moved away from. We've learned to be cautious of volunteer trainees who have served the same role in a different place; more often than not they will try to change ECCO procedures and end up disrupting the area they work in.

When working with out-of-town volunteers at Charleston Outreach, we provided extensive orientation weekends, better known as "Train the Trainer." We trained group leaders to train out-of-town volunteers. These out-of-town volunteers would return home and prepare their churches to come minister in Charleston. From the information we gave, group leaders would base weeklong mission trips to train their volunteers, both youth and adults, for the opportunity ahead. We provided a time for basic orientation about Charleston and the needs we had. Then we would break out into training classes for the different types of ministry the volunteers had selected. The next morning was a windshield tour of the many different ministries, locations, and settings.

A volunteer job description helps alleviate misunderstandings and expectations of both the organization and the volunteer. For example, our food pantry requires less training than those who serve as front-line volunteers. Job descriptions describe the function and responsibilities of the position; they lay out what a volunteer is responsible for and who they are responsible to.

COMMITMENT OF TIME

At ECCO, a huge challenge was to discover volunteer availability and commitment. Volunteers must know up front what time will be required to serve in the role of interest. Since we have so many types of programs, the requirements vary from position to position. Our normal routine for the food pantry is for volunteers to serve in three-hour shifts, either in the morning or afternoon. Dentists volunteer one shift a month in the dental clinic. Instructors may serve an hour per week.

Since we live in a resort area, we find a lot of volunteers who live here half the year and live back home the other half. Thirty percent of the volunteer force is made up of retirees who live in East Cooper during the winter and return in the summer months to their homes or vacation homes in the north. These are people committed to our mission but who are only in town and available for service during the winter months. Knowing this up front allows planning and preparation for their absence during the summer months.

MAINTAINING VOLUNTEERS

To lead volunteers to be the most efficient and effective they can be, they must understand how their work ties into the mission of the organization. The keys to maintaining volunteers include appreciation, celebration, and evaluation.

APPRECIATION

American philosopher William James said, "The deepest principle in human nature is the craving to be appreciated."

Everyone wants to be appreciated. Appreciation can be shown in all kinds of ways. We recognize the Volunteer of the Month with e-blasts, newsletters, and plaques. Pins are awarded for years of service, and most volunteers pin them on their name tag lanyards. The month of April is National Volunteer Appreciation Month, and we provide lunch and take two hours to celebrate during both morning and afternoon shifts. During this gathering, volunteers share their backgrounds and the most rewarding experience they recently encountered. Recently we created an annual stakeholders meeting where we present the annual statistics of the outputs of each program.

ONGOING TRAINING

Ongoing training helps keep volunteers up to date on the procedures of the organization and serves as a means to help them feel more connected. Training sessions are held to better their understanding of the data system used for helping our clients. This builds their confidence and shows how they are personally involved in improving the lives of our clients. Other training sessions include customer service, interview skills, and updates from partnering organizations, to name a few.

EVALUATION

Evaluation is important to the individual and the organization. The organization should conduct these annually, and making the evaluation part of the job description makes it easier for all parties involved. Volunteers want to know how they're doing, and the organization likes the insight provided and the resulting flexibility to make changes—to make volunteers more effective and efficient. If needed, reassignments can help both parties. The volunteer and the organization could both be uncomfortable in the current situation—the individual may not feel comfortable or fulfilled in their assignment, and the organization may not like the performance of the person in the role they assume.

CELEBRATION

We celebrate the service of our volunteers during our annual Stone Soup gala. In this informal setting we present three awards: one for longevity; one for the "superhero" who shows up at a moment's notice; and the Stone Soup Award, our most prestigious award, which I mentioned earlier as being for the person who has made the most significant contribution to ECCO.

We also recognize our volunteers in the spring with a cookout to thank them for their contribution to our mission. This is a very casual affair that takes place on a small island in the intracoastal waterway.

Volunteers, when properly recruited, trained, and managed, are integral to the life of a nonprofit. Their assistance multiplies the work of the staff, and in many instances, they can serve as if they are a staff. We are fortunate to have, at times, volunteers outnumbering staff twenty to one. Case in point is the work of

Sue and Ernie Brown, who moved to Charleston from Kentucky with Charleston Outreach. They had both retired and felt called to serve in their later years. Sue served full time, working in three multi-housing communities while Ernie worked full time in our construction ministry, which rehabbed houses in the inner city. Sue and Ernie came to staff meetings and all the activities that were part of our year-round program. I remember Sue saying, "Jack, this is what we worked so hard for all of our lives. We have been so blessed by serving the needs of others."

Monsignor Carter receives the first Stone Soup Award.

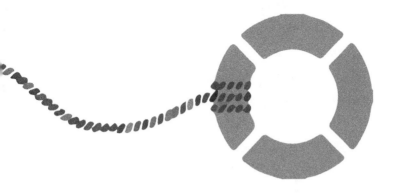

CHAPTER 10
Programs

One of the most memorable times of my life was when my children were young. We read and played together, indoors and out. Inside, we played with building blocks, creating castles and towers while learning some basic life skills such as how blocks fit together to construct tall towers and walls. To build vertically, we learned, we had to have a strong foundation.

Building programs to help the poor and working poor move into financial independence is a lot like that. Strong foundations must be constructed to enable continued building and growing. In 2005, ECCO had basic programs for emergency assistance of food and clothing, and its health programs included a simple dental emergency extraction service and a prescription assistance program. Building quality programs atop these platforms was the opportunity that lay ahead.

Please note the previous chapter shows the value of our volunteers. In this chapter, a value has been placed on each program. This will vividly show the difference ECCO makes in our community and how nonprofit groups operate more efficiently than government agencies.

The programs ECCO provides the underserved are numerous; we strive to offer every service needed to assist our clients, resulting in tremendous growth with a strategic process to assist the poor. In the beginning, we responded only to the requested need. For instance, if someone came in for food, that's what they received. If they needed assistance with their prescription, that's what we helped them with. Today, we try to meet client needs across a spectrum of services with a comprehensive assessment of every area of their life. Our programs are divided into three categories: Basic Needs, Health and Nutrition, and Empowerment. I'll break these categories down in detail, but for now, let's summarize them.

Basic Needs is the core program that supports families in poverty by providing food, clothing, household goods, and emergency financial assistance. This program area remains a critical component of the organization's overall operation—delivery of basic safety-net services is a major reason why more than fifty individuals per day visit the facility for help. Through the intake process, their individual needs are fully assessed to determine any additional program opportunities that could help them rise out of poverty.

Health services focuses on helping the uninsured and under-insured by providing emergency prescription medication assistance and education, healthy eating and wellness classes, counseling, preventive and restorative dental care, emergency extractions, and ongoing health maintenance and medical care. Access to health care has long been listed as an important factor in an individual's likelihood of getting out of poverty.

Empowerment comprises the most comprehensive strategy for clients to achieve increased education and financial literacy. With a sustainable approach to poverty elimination, our programs Getting Ahead and ECCO Works focus on overcoming obstacles, personal advancement, and setting goals to reach self-sufficiency. The Getting Ahead program is for single mothers in need and provides group support and mentorship to help participants build confidence and discover new life possibilities. ECCO Works is designed for unemployed and underemployed adults and incorporates soft skills for job readiness, case management, and connections to employers. We also provide Individual Development Accounts (IDA), a savings-match program to help build their assets.

SECTION 1: BASIC NEEDS

In 2008, when we began to venture into helping people become financially independent, the board agreed to hire case managers and front office staff. Board members realized the advantages of having a professional, dependable office staff to complete the analytical assessments and services our clients need. This was a huge step in serving our clients more holistically. The challenge was to provide an effective, seamless, streamlined approach to capture the varied needs of each individual.

FOOD AND CLOTHING

ECCO began by providing food and clothing, as these were the genesis of our services offered after Hurricane Hugo. The warehouse ministries have morphed through the years, supplying thousands of people with emergency food and clothing. Over time, changes have been made to be more efficient to better serve the client.

In 2014, ECCO provided food for 5,825 families who were food deficient. With a three-day supply for each family, that equated to 342,450 pounds. The food warehouse resembles a grocery store of sorts; it consists of four aisles of grocery store-style shelves. The usual staple items are included in our menu. Canned meats, vegetables, cereals, peanut butter, pasta, eggs, bread, and toiletries are given out. Even dog and cat food are offered. Over the years, the food options have become healthier, as we have moved to a health initiative in helping our clients become more aware of their own personal nutrition. On top of daily food provisions, ECCO provides more than five hundred turkey dinners to help low-income families at Thanksgiving. These efforts are possible because we strive to maintain a fully stocked warehouse of more than four thousand square feet.

FOOD SUPPLIERS

Our most reliable source for food is the community, through our local churches. More than thirty area churches conduct a food drive called Grocery Bag Sunday; some organize them once a year while others hold them once a quarter. Paper grocery bags with a list of needed items stapled to them are distributed to church members. The bags are filled with items on the lists and then brought back to the church the following Sunday. The church then brings the bags to ECCO the following day. Sixty percent of the food collected through the year is from the local churches.

Throughout the summer, subdivisions also collect food. Neighborhood Homeowners Association leaders promote the cause. Demand is particularly high during the summer months. Kids home from school are not receiving free lunches, and the responsibility falls on the summer feeding programs. Larger subdivisions are broken down into smaller areas, with team captains posting and distributing the fliers

Caitlyn Dunleavy helped organize a food drive for children who did not have lunch during the summer.

about the program to the community. Residents bring food to a central location to be collected and delivered or picked up by ECCO.

A consistent source of food is local grocery stores. Our next-door neighbor is Harris Teeter. This store donates its bakery's daily overages. BI-LO, another grocer, contributes a daily vanload of overstocked items and items with recent or upcoming expiration dates.

The balance comes from the local food bank. Their supply depends on what becomes available to them. Even though their selections are limited, their supply fills out the rest of our inventory.

QUALIFYING

Our criteria for service require people to live in the East Cooper area, but no one is turned away. If a person comes to our facility and asks for food, they get it regardless.

It takes a lot of humility to come to ask for assistance. I have seen too many people come with heavy hearts and their hats in their hand. If they live out of our service area, we serve them at least one time and then encourage them to seek future food assistance in their community. We provide the names and locations of the pantries in their area to assist them in finding a more convenient location.

PROCESS

The policy for the frequency of food assistance is once every thirty days. We want to avoid creating a dependency of outside help, although exceptions are made in special situations. Every client is interviewed by a volunteer, who then assists the client with their food selection on a computer screen. Because the supply of food changes each day, a daily morning inventory is taken to provide a current list of available foods. Our method of service empowers rather than enables, so we allow clients to select their own food from a daily updated grocery list. When referring to enabling, we're talking about a behavior of dependency whereas empowering creates independence. The experience not only allows a more hospitable atmosphere for the client but also has a deeper impact, allowing them to be in control of the choices they learn to make in our health and nutrition classes.

The impact of our food program is more than $750,000.

CLOTHING

East Cooper is a wealthy community. Though our territory is mostly rural, there is a lot of wealth in the Town of Mount Pleasant, as well as on Daniel Island, Isle of Palms, and Sullivan's Island. People from the north are finding this is a great place to retire. Wealthy businesspeople live in this resort area and commute to New York, Chicago, and Atlanta.

The effect of this has an overflow effect on ECCO. We receive donations of clothing and furniture that is above the norm. A lot of us would be happy to claim these items as our own. We could build fashionable wardrobes and furnish our homes in style. We do receive the normal dirty and worn clothing as well, but these are sought out and put aside to recycle.

Several years ago, I knew something could be done with these unfit clothing items to generate revenue for us. After searching for a couple of months I discovered a company in Florida that recycles rags and clothing. They agreed to put a forty-foot tractor-trailer unit in our side yard. When we fill it, they pick it up, weigh it, and pay us by the pound. We receive almost $3,000 per year from this arrangement.

Approved clothing is taken to the clothing area, where it is put out for our clients to choose from. The space looks like a normal clothing store, with garments organized into sizes and colors. More than six hundred clients are served per month in this area.

One Thursday afternoon, a graduate of our job readiness class came in needing clothing for an interview. The volunteers working that afternoon began helping her choose interview outfits. As they were putting together several outfits, they discovered she had children, so they also began collecting clothing for her children.

Their efforts impacted not only the client's life but also their own—they felt they had been involved in a fulfilling act of mercy. That evening, one of the volunteers went home and told her husband. He was vice president and general manager for a manufacturing plant in the area. After I heard this, I approached him about serving on our board. The story his wife told him convinced him of the importance of ECCO, so he agreed to join the board. Today, he is our president. When he joined the board, he also brought the workforce from his plant. He, his wife, and his company have made significant financial contributions to ECCO over the years. It is difficult to put a value on our clothing, but if placed at the value of Goodwill Industries, it would be more than $210,000.

SECTION 2: HEALTH SERVICES

ECCO's focus on health and wellness is a key contribution to the community. Almost 20 percent of our area residents don't have medical or dental insurance; many area residents already have or are at risk for developing long-term medical issues such as heart disease, stroke, diabetes, or hypertension. Taking the necessary steps to educate those at risk is critical in helping to prevent them from developing diseases and ending up in need of treatment but lacking adequate insurance to cover doctor's visits or medication. The potential long-term impact could result in decreasing the number of medical and dental visits and hopefully influencing positive change in future generations.

The overall goal of ECCO's health services program is for clients to experience an improvement in their physical and/or mental well-being and to learn how to make healthier lifestyle choices. The staff focus on personal health responsibility and accountability, supported by client education and long-term follow-up. If treatment plans are followed, the long-term health benefits help to reduce conditions that already exist. Across ECCO's many programs is an integrated focus of personal health responsibility and empowerment, which is only possible by teaching clients how to prepare regular and affordable nutritious meals. The benefit of offering health education is that it encourages long-term, systemic changes toward a healthy lifestyle, which are supplemented by ongoing case management and free dental and medical care.

DENTAL SERVICES

The ECCO dental clinic has become a statewide model for other clinics. It offers almost the full range of services a professional practice has.

Beginning with the dental clinic founded in 1991 as an emergency extraction clinic, today ECCO furnishes a very broad array of health services. What began as a single dental chair in a single-wide trailer parked next to ECCO's warehouse—where dentists extracted decaying and abscessed teeth on Tuesday and

Thursday evenings—has become a forty-hour-a-week, state-of-the art clinic performing more than three thousand procedures each year.

We knew regular preventive oral hygiene may limit or prevent abscessed teeth, heart disease, pre-term and low-birth-weight babies, and diabetes, so expanding our services was necessary. We discovered the third most common reason for hospital emergency room visits are for toothaches. The American Dental Association has stated that in most cases, patients who present at an emergency department with a nontraumatic dental condition would be better served in a dental office setting due to the availability of definitive care and the likelihood of continuity care.

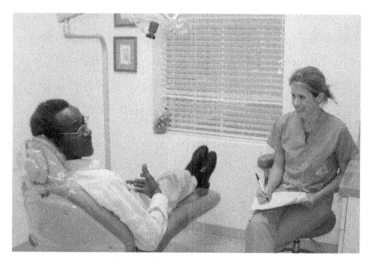

Because the dental clinic operated during the evening hours after the warehouse had closed for the day, a stigma was created that ECCO and the dental clinic worked independently, like two different organizations. Even when the new building was built, the dental clinic was on one side of the lobby and the offices and warehouse were on the other. It was like an "us" and "them" mentality. The problem was exacerbated when volunteer gatherings included both the food and warehouse volunteers because the dental volunteers were overlooked. Through many years and different dental directors, the separation was overcome when Leslie White, our current manager, came onboard. She initiated better organizational relationships by coming to the office area daily to talk and chat with other employees.

In 2006, being a "newbie" to the nonprofit world, I was looking for new funding to grow ECCO in the way God was leading. My brother-in-law, who worked for Blue Cross Blue Shield in another state, told me about each state division having its own foundation dedicated to improving health for the underserved. So I made an appointment with the president of the Blue Cross Blue Shield of South Carolina Foundation, Harvey Galloway, and went to Columbia to meet with him.

This experience was not one of the highlights of my career. Walking onto the Blue Cross Blue Shield grounds was like going into a huge kingdom. The buildings were bigger than life, with high-tech security, and there was a cafeteria just outside the lobby. I registered, and a lady named Nancy came down the elevator to escort me back upstairs to meet with Galloway. I walked down a long hallway into Nancy's office and waited for him to call me in.

When he told Nancy over the intercom to bring me in, I had a panic attack. My mouth froze, and trying to tell him about ECCO and our needs was one of the hardest challenges of my life. I had met with state and corporate leaders before in my former life and never had this happen. I struggled through my spiel about ECCO expanding to provide restorative dental care and waited for Galloway to respond to the worst presentation in my life.

He made me feel at ease and told me to call him Harvey. He had looked at our website and told me how intriguing our organization was. I shared with him the history of ECCO and the current emergency dental extraction clinic. I explained how we wanted to take the clinic to the next level and provide restorative care by providing fillings and trying to save teeth rather than extracting them. He understood how this would better serve the long-term needs of the people we served. He invited ECCO to apply for a grant and began explaining the application process.

Back home, we began the process of making an application. The criteria for the restorative clinic would be that the patients had to live in the East Cooper area, be uninsured, and have a household income of less than 200 percent of the poverty level. This was a stark contrast from the emergency clinic, where we had no criteria for the service. The change of requirements came because our volunteer dentists were concerned they might lose their patients to us. We had thirty-five volunteer dentists working in the evening emergency extraction clinic, and we didn't want to upset them to the point that they would stop providing service. We finished the grant application and submitted it. A few months later the phone rang during our health care meeting, of all meetings. We only had five employees at the time, so when the office manager came and told me I had a call from Harvey, I ran to the phone, where I was congratulated. "Jack," Harvey said, "Blue Cross Blue Shield of South Carolina Foundation has awarded ECCO the full amount that was requested of $50,000!" I ran back into the meeting and told everyone, and they all stood and clapped. It was the first major grant ECCO had ever received, and it was the beginning of ECCO's growth.

In 2007, the clinic began offering fillings due to the grant from Blue Cross Blue Shield of South Carolina Foundation. The clinic began opening in the mornings and afternoons, and the number of people served grew tremendously. Our dental facility is now state of the art. It contains high-tech equipment with four operatory rooms, each with a standard reclining patient chair, overhead lights, dental equipment and drills, high-volume suction, water hoses, digital X-ray equipment, and a panoramic X-ray machine. This allows us to provide our clients first-class service and gives our clients a sense of dignity and worth.

In 2010, we began offering preventive care on a consistent basis, but as we did this, we suddenly realized that we could not provide cleanings because the state of South Carolina demands that a patient have a complete oral examination performed by a licensed dentist in the prior year. Most of our clients had never had their teeth cleaned. So we were granted funding by Blue Cross Blue Shield of South Carolina Foundation for funding for a part-time dental hygienist. We were able to assist more than three hundred patients with this service in the first year.

We first utilized local dentists who could volunteer during daytime hours. These were few because most of them had their own practices to run during those hours, so we began looking for retired dentists in the area. We were lucky and found a couple who could help us. Like most retirees who have moved to Charleston, the couple hadn't renewed their licenses, so we offered to pay for their renewals. This allowed us to perform the examinations until one of the dentists became ill and the other relocated to Georgia.

While that was upsetting, we soon realized that one of our volunteer dental students had graduated and wanted to stay in the area. We hired her to work for us one day a week; the rest of the week she worked in practices in other towns in the area. We began scheduling the clients for oral examinations the one day she was available.

This worked well until she married and relocated to Greenville, South Carolina, leaving us to scramble for another solution. God then provided for us again by bringing another dentist retiree to our community. Dr. Michael Cuenin was a retired Army periodontist. His job in the service was to begin dental clinics in camps around the world for our troops abroad—perfect!

A dental student with Executive Director Jack Little.

The next service we began offering was partial dentures for our clients. These were folks who had experienced tooth loss or who had teeth extracted but were not insured. They were not able to afford the high cost of partial dentures. Partials are important because they provide a number of health and mental benefits. Recipients are able to chew their food more completely, for one thing. Also, in addition to the benefits of proper dental care and oral health, having a mouthful of teeth and a healthy smile can provide a person living in poverty a sense of self-worth and can boost confidence during a job interview. ECCO's dental clinic is the only dental clinic in the state that provides partials to clients for free, which is an innovative addition to addressing the targeted health priority. Priority is given to those in the ECCO Works program to help them enhance their confidence as they apply for jobs. This is another way our wraparound services embrace our clients.

Blue Cross Blue Shield of South Carolina Foundation provided funding for three years, resulting in a total of more than twenty-one thousand free procedures for seven thousand patients. The clinic staff produced partial dentures for fifty clients during the first twelve months. In 2016, we will increase to sixty clients per year. Through this program, we

Harvey Galloway announces a grant for the dental clinic from Blue Cross Blue Shield Foundation of SC.

anticipate helping 250 new clients for preventive and restorative care and will continue to serve about two thousand returning clients.

As part of ECCO's overall strategic mission to provide comprehensive services for clients that will have a long-term impact and encourage self-sufficiency, an increased focus on health education has been incorporated into our dental, medical, and food programs. We offer monthly classes for adults that cover a variety of health- and food-related subjects, such as cooking and walking and teaching adults how to utilize their financial resources in the grocery store.

Here is a client's success story from ECCO's Spring Newsletter 2012:

ECCO DENTAL CLINIC CREATES BEAUTIFUL NEW SMILE

Hello Friends and Faculty of the East Cooper Outreach Center!

My name is Cynthia Cole, and I wanted to share that, thanks to "My Sister's Smile," our program for battered women, and its caring, amazing staff, I have made it through an extremely difficult period in my life and have begun a very exciting new chapter. I am able to be social again, have started to enjoy life again, and, most of all, smile with confidence!

My problem started about twelve years ago, when I began grinding my teeth without realizing the extent of the damage that the grinding was causing. I eventually ended up with exposed nerves in what little of the teeth remained. I also had to have teeth pulled because the chipping was so bad my teeth were into the sides of my cheeks.

Each time that I looked in the mirror, I would cringe at how my mouth looked, and I felt so ashamed to talk or even smile. I became less and less social, until I isolated myself from everyone except my closest friends. It hurt me so badly that I could not smile in pictures with my friends, family, or especially, my grandchildren, without feeling embarrassed.

When I first learned I was grinding my teeth from one dentist and how much the dental restoration would cost ... I was shocked. I have been out of work, and it has been impossible to get a job, because, as we all know, appearance and first impressions are so important. I tried everything to find a person or an organization that would help—all with no luck! So I went from a vibrant, joyful, smiling social butterfly to one who felt she had no hope left.

By the Grace of God and a close friend, I was introduced to Dr. McEniry and his wonderful staff at "My Sister's Smile." I spoke with Dr. McEniry and Dina Walker, and I was quickly worked into their very tight schedule when they discovered the severity

Cynthia Cole [L] after her smile was restored.

of my condition. I was so ashamed at how my teeth looked and thought I would be judged for allowing such a thing to happen. I felt amazingly at ease with the wonderful staff and was not at all judged by my misfortune! "My Sister's Smile" restored my confidence and my smile!

Thanks to Dr. McEniry, his ministry, and the amazing, caring staff associated with "My Sister's Smile," I am at a wonderful, exciting new place in my life! Please let the pictures help you know how important this program is to such good people in need, and that it can only be provided to us through donations from all of you!

I would like to thank Dr. McEniry, Dr. Sasser, Dina Walker, Leslie White, Drema Lindeman, and all the caring people whose donations help make this program available!

Special thanks also to Merri, who has been my guidance and a true friend through it all!!!

Sincerely,

Cynthia L. Cole

Last year, the impact of the dental clinic was $1.1 million.

HEALTH AND WELLNESS

People on limited budgets often think of health care as their last priority. Unless a sudden illness or virus strikes, a doctor's visit is the least likely scheduled appointment. Before 2008, ECCO's health approach was to be reactive and not proactive, and responding to illnesses and diseases was our practice. We still see those who have episodic occurrences, but our first priority today is the promotion of healthy lifestyles. Health education and exercise classes are being offered. Nutrition and healthy eating courses have been well received. Our challenge is to help our clients break though the habits learned through generations of poverty, but public awareness created through the mainstream media has made the general public receptive to this new way of thinking. We find the low-income population just doesn't have the opportunities to learn and/or the knowledge most people have.

When a new client comes to ECCO, our intake/assessment case manager conducts a thorough needs assessment to determine eligibility before referring the client to the health and wellness manager or scheduling them for an appointment for the dental clinic, prescription assistance program (PAP), or Partners in HealthCare.

There is a critical community need for those individuals living in poverty to have access to dental and health care. Approximately 20 percent of the households in ECCO's service area have no health insurance. It's important to note that our service area has the country's highest prevalence of heart disease, stroke, obesity, diabetes, and infant mortality, conditions that can be exacerbated by poor or nonexistent dental and health care. Many

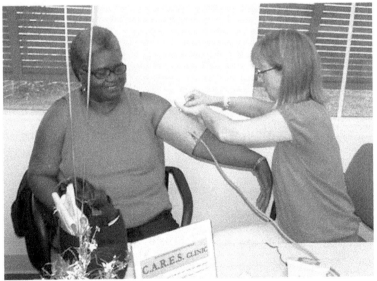

factors contribute to the plight of the poor and uninsured. The lack of transportation is a factor, since we serve a largely rural area. Our residents also have a deep-rooted cultural belief that accepts hypertension, diabetes, hyperlipidemia (high cholesterol), and tooth loss as normal and inevitable. Inadequate information about these chronic conditions also contributes to the low priority for personal care. As a result, our low-income neighbors are unlikely to seek medical or dental care unless serious problems exist.

ECCO has responded to this serious breach of services by having an almost complete array of health care services. The first service offered was the dental clinic, followed by our prescription assistance program and health clinics. Since we changed our focus to empowering rather than enabling people, we changed the framework of our health services to educating clients to be proactive in their health care. Preventative education programs—classes on living with and averting these conditions—have also added to our menu of health services.

Poor eating habits not only come from not knowing but also from the limited amount of money that people in poverty earn. Southern cooking is one of the worst techniques of cooking in the world. Fried chicken, vegetables cooked with fatback, macaroni and cheese, and biscuits have been the staples of consumption for the past 150 years. Our nutrition and cooking lessons teach that natural foods prepared with natural spices can be appetizing and tasty.

A six-week class that we hold in collaboration of the Low-country Food Bank teaches this kind of cooking. Called "Cooking Matters," this class provides hands-on instruction for preparing healthy and affordable meals. For two hours a week, the interactive course covers menu planning, budgeting, cooking methods, knife safety, and health benefits.

Participants cook in every class, go home with a bag of food after each class, and receive gifts upon graduation. The class also includes a trip to the grocery store to teach how to shop healthy by staying on the perimeter of the store. A voucher of $25 is given to participants to shop as they have been taught. Each class has been filled to capacity.

Cooking class at ECCO

In recent years, ECCO has also started numerous health education initiatives that, in 2014 alone, engaged more than 170 participants. Through a number of partnerships, ECCO has been able to offer other wellness classes such as walking and yoga to promote exercise and stress relief.

The Living Well program was designed for people with ongoing health conditions, such as arthritis, diabetes, asthma or other breathing problems, heart disease, and high blood pressure. These chronic conditions require learning important self-management tools to help people take control of their health. Participants came one night per week and walked two miles at the adjacent school across the street. After meeting at ECCO and a pep talk from our instructor, they would walk and return to discuss their personal performance and encourage their classmates. This interactive workshop was designed so that participants can meet, encourage, and learn from others.

The purpose of the REACH Diabetes class, offered through Prescription Assistance, was to eliminate health disparities related to diabetes prevention and control by reducing risks and preventing complications of diabetes related to hypertension, stroke, and amputations. Classes were held for five consecutive weeks.

EMERGENCY PRESCRIPTION ASSISTANCE PROGRAM

After closing late one Friday afternoon, a lady knocked on our doors loud enough to get my attention. I answered the door, and she told me her mother had just been released from the hospital and she came to ECCO because the hospital staff told them about our emergency prescription assistance program. I told her we were closed and she would have to come back Monday morning. She began pleading with me because her mother was in dire pain. To verify her mother's need, I walked out to the car, where I saw an elderly woman writhing in pain. It was heart wrenching. I invited the daughter back in, and I began filling out the paperwork for us to assist her that day.

Stories abound of people not being able to afford their medications and include stories about the elderly and disabled not taking their medications as prescribed because of economic hardship. I heard of an elderly homebound lady who would cut her pills into two pieces and take one every other day, when the prescription called for her to take one a day.

Hoyt Kiser is assisted by a physician at the clinic.

Emergency prescription assistance (EPA) covers supplementary medical services that require prescriptions for medications, laboratory and radiology diagnostics, mammograms, vision testing, and glasses. Roper St. Francis Health Foundation (RSFHF) funds are also used to purchase emergency prescriptions (usually a thirty-day supply) for clients who are unable to pay. Our staff shops local pharmacies for the best price on each prescription, and we pay for the thirty-day supply so that the patient may receive their medication and start treatment immediately. This prevents having any drugs on our premises. The EPA program is especially important to our newly established Partners in HealthCare program (to be discussed later) because one of the clinic's focuses is on chronic disease management to treat patients experiencing hypertension, hyperlipidemia, and diabetes.

When a client has a chronic health problem, staff works to enroll them into our prescription assistance program (PAP), where we connect with pharmaceutical companies. Support from RSFHF is also used to provide for staff support for this service so that clients can receive support for long-term medication maintenance. The prescription assistance office provides the coordination required between client, physician, and pharmaceutical company for enrollment in the PAPs through an application process. While the paperwork is being approved, emergency prescription assistance is provided to clients on a one-time basis. The client receives education on the importance of following their medication regimen and keeping doctor appointments to reduce the amount of emergency room visits. During 2013, ECCO filled more than six hundred emergency prescriptions; the cost to ECCO was only $18,846, and there was no cost to the clients. This includes 134 new clients and 311 in total.

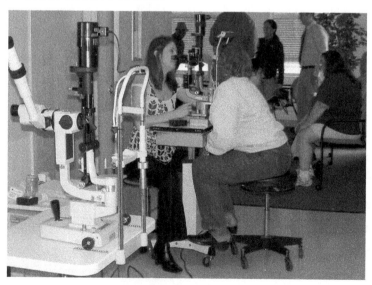

LABORATORY DIAGNOSIS ASSISTANCE

In 2007, we approached Father Terry Reynolds, the missions director of Roper St. Francis Hospital, about partnering with the prescription program. He went to the hospital's foundation, and they agreed to supplement the prescriptions assistance position. RSFHF also agreed to provide diagnostic lab and radiology analyses for our clients, when referred by our health and wellness manager. A client visit to a free clinic often results in a prescription for a blood workup or an X-ray. With no insurance, these tests can be prohibitively expensive, and lack of testing can be a serious impediment to developing appropriate patient treatment plans.

The annual value of our prescription assistance program, including health education and nutrition classes and lab testing, is $791,000.

PARTNERS IN HEALTHCARE

Partners in HealthCare, ECCO's newest health services initiative grew from a pilot program that was started in April 2013 to address specific health concerns that had been identified among our clients. For years, ECCO had searched for ways to involve nurses in our work. In 2010, a retired nurse, Dianne Schuler, became a member of our board. She felt her purpose was just that. Her perseverance led her to meet and pursue instructors from the College of Nursing at MUSC. In 2013, ECCO piloted a nurse practitioner program to serve the health care needs of East Cooper residents.

The opening of Partners in Healthcare [L to R] Msgr Carter, Mayor Linda Page, Board President, Giff Daughtridge, and the chair of MUSC Family Practice, Dr. Terry Steyer.

After collecting patient data for one year, three prevalent issues were determined as the most critical—diabetes, hypertension, and hyperlipidemia. Evaluating the pilot program's results and receiving feedback from ECCO's clients led to officially launching the Partners in HealthCare clinic as a permanent service. Partners in HealthCare has already demonstrated its effectiveness and made an impact. Since introducing the nurse practitioner clinic, there have been 408 patient visits, tracked with the following diagnoses: 37 percent overweight or obese, 47 percent diabetic, 79 percent hypertensive, and 68 percent with hyperlipidemia. Initial results show that since visiting the clinic, only 8 percent have gone once to the emergency room, and only 4 percent have had one hospital admission—compared to an average of six ER visits for the uninsured with chronic diseases.

Partners in Healthcare's annual community impact is $89,000.

SECTION 3: EMPOWERMENT

When I hear people say that the word "empowerment" doesn't have a clear, concise meaning, I realize that they are saying, "Empowerment is sort of a mushy word." The term is better understood when it is put in the context of enabling someone to do something they couldn't do on their own.

Empowerment is a hard word to get a firm understanding of, but let's look at it this way. I recall a story about a father who came home after his workday and saw his four-year-old son playing basketball. He saw that his son was not even getting close to the basketball goal net, much less the rim, with each shot. The dad got out of his car and started playing with his son. He instructed his son how to use the strength of his body to get more power behind his shot. The boy kept shooting but could never sink a shot or even get close to the rim. Soon, the dad realized his son couldn't do it on his own. So he picked up the boy and put him on his shoulders, gave him the ball to let him try. On the first attempt, the boy made the shot. The son was ecstatic! He made it!

This story is a great description of the term "empowerment." It's helping someone achieve something they couldn't do on their own. ECCO has the necessary tools for someone to build a platform to secure a beginning and to then launch themselves into a hopeful future.

OUT OF POVERTY INITIATIVE

Previously, I spoke of our community-wide effort to combat poverty in the East Cooper communities. After hearing educator and author Ruby Payne speak, I read and distributed the book she coauthored, *Bridges Out of Poverty*, to our board.

A couple of months later, I made contact with Philip DeVol, one of three coauthors of the book, about beginning a career center at ECCO. I knew that poverty could only be overcome through people earning a livable wage, so I had been researching employment workforce development programs. When I told DeVol my thoughts and plans and I asked what other initiatives we should begin focusing on, he asked what other organizations were involved in my effort. When I told him no one else was involved, he told me to "stop right there." He explained that one organization could not do everything to eliminate poverty and that we had to involve other organizations, businesses, government agencies, and churches in the effort. My zeal was halted in its tracks. I knew he was right.

The next spring, we hosted our first seminar for the tri-county area (about 650,000 population), inviting community leaders, churches, government agencies, and nonprofits. Terri Drussie Smith, another coauthor of *Bridges Out of Poverty*, led a discussion on "The Hidden Rules of Economic Class." Over 120 people participated in the meeting; it was so successful we sponsored two more in the following couple of years. The conference taught that the best practices for addressing underserved communities was to assess personal and community resources. This is the opposite of the common practices used by most social service and governmental agencies. The usual practice is to find the needs and deficits of a community and fill the voids. Most of the general public views the underserved communities as having no assets and attempts to fill those for the community. The key word here is "for"—these folks set up food pantries and clothes closets trying to help the poor. When "do-gooders" do things "for" the needy, they have no skin in the game. Consequently, residents resent those efforts, feeling that they degrade their human ability to take control of their lives. They strip the individual and the community of their personal dignity.

Studies have shown that where you find these services, you find a poor community that is dependent on others—government agencies, churches, and charities—to fill their needs. The community never rises above its present, depressed condition. In North Charleston, depressed communities are filled with competing charities offering the same services within blocks of one another.

The principles learned from Smith were applied in a strategic way. We named our effort "The Out of Poverty Initiative" (OOPI). The initiative sought to address generational poverty throughout our service region, including the historically African American settlement communities in East Cooper and in the outlying rural communities within the ECCO service area. Our goals were to empower participants through education, financial literacy, and asset-building programs. Over the years, I have learned to listen and hear the needs and wishes of the people. Scores of community needs assessments were conducted throughout my career to help us understand where we needed to begin. To accomplish this in East Cooper, we gathered leaders from the heirs' property communities together and formed a coalition called "Communities Organized to Realize Excellence" (CORE). We asked the leaders to reach out to their community residents through a survey and find their interest and concerns. The survey revealed the top five areas of the greatest concern: access to health care services, affordable housing, drug and alcohol prevention, mentoring for children and youth, and job training for adults.

The community outreach efforts of the OOPI began focusing on systemic change by raising the awareness of the community, identifying the root causes of poverty, and engaging the community to address identified barriers.

Mount Pleasant Presbyterian Church had a member observing. Al Jenkins heard these needs. He led his church in starting a program to mentor at-risk primary school kids though their elementary school years. There was an immediate impact, as conduct and grades improved. Five more churches enlisted volunteers to serve three more schools. In 2015, four schools had more than 250 students involved, served by over 450 volunteers; the volunteers meet with their child once a week at lunchtime to practice the child's reading skills.

GETTING AHEAD

The original effort of the OOPI was to begin the "Getting Ahead" workshops in 2009. Getting Ahead takes a multifaceted approach to generational poverty by focusing on the needs of the entire family, rather than just an individual. This fifteen-week workshop was developed to involve single mothers from the age of twenty to forty-five. The class is composed of fifteen sessions and teaches critical thinking, situation analysis, goal setting, and planning skills. Participants are provided with books and materials, instruction, a meal, free babysitting, and also receive a small stipend for their class participation. Each participant graduates with a personally designed plan for self-improvement that includes three attainable goals.

The program provides participants guidance, support, and motivation, even after the completion of the course. Participants are paired with a trained mentor to connect them with resources to help them achieve their goals. Graduates of Getting Ahead are intensively case managed for three to five years; they are offered counseling services and receive priority for emergency financial assistance in order to stabilize the family situation. To date, more than two hundred women have been through the program and 75 percent of them either have gone back to school or got new jobs or promotions.

The first step toward financial independence is linking members to safety-net services—like food, health care, and assistance with paying for utilities and rent or mortgage—to support the family while participants realize their personally designed plan for self-improvement. Participants are also screened for eligibility for Temporary Assistance for Needy Families (TANF) and Supplemental Nutritional Assistance Program (SNAP) benefits. It's important for people who struggle to maximize available benefits to help their families survive.

After immediate needs are met, the program encourages financial independence through further education/empowerment and asset-building programs, including parenting workshops, financial literacy courses for adults and children, self-esteem workshops, resume-writing workshops, credit-counseling courses, work readiness courses, and homework help for school-age children. The family is provided continual support, guidance, and safety-net services throughout their transition out of poverty to a more sustainable life.

Based on feedback from the participants in our early programs, ECCO has begun offering additional education programs. Starting in January 2010, ECCO began offering motivated clients the opportunity to participate in the financial literacy class, Money Smart.

INDIVIDUAL DEVELOPMENT ACCOUNTS (IDA)

One of the most common root causes of poverty is the lack of financial resources and assets. When you live paycheck to paycheck it's almost impossible to ever build any surplus for savings; few have any savings, and most do not know how to save. The lifestyle and decision-making processes of the poor also do not bode well for their future. For many, the tendency is to spend now, enjoy the moment, and worry later. Many purchase basic necessities and then use any remaining money to make large, expensive purchases like a car, new flat screen TV, or elaborate sound system. This lifestyle and spending habits were normally learned from their parents, who learned from their parents.

ECCO also began offering financial literacy class graduates the option of participating in the ECCO Savings Match program, which I mentioned earlier. This federally funded Individual Development Account (IDA) program earns participants a three-to-one match on their deposited stipends until they reach $1,000 in their accounts, $4,000 with the match. The funds are restricted and can only be used to buy a house, continue their education, or start a business.

The IDA program is the most effective program available to help someone in poverty build assets. It is part of the Assets for Independence Act, which was created to help the working poor build assets. The Act states that:

(1) Economic well-being does not come solely from income, spending, and consumption, but also requires savings, investment, and accumulation of assets because assets can improve economic independence and stability, connect individuals with a viable and hopeful future, stimulate development of human and other capital, and enhance the welfare of offspring.

(2) Fully one-half of all Americans have either no, negligible, or negative assets available for investment, just as the price of entry to the economic mainstream, the cost of a house, an adequate education, and starting a business, is increasing. Further, the household savings rate of the United States lags far behind other industrial nations, presenting a barrier to economic growth.

(3) In the current tight fiscal environment, the United States should invest existing resources in high-yield initiatives. There is reason to believe that the financial returns, including increased income, tax revenue, and decreased welfare cash assistance, resulting from Individual Development Accounts will far exceed the cost of investment in those accounts.

(4) Traditional public assistance programs concentrating on income and consumption have rarely been successful in promoting and supporting the transition

to increased economic self-sufficiency. Income-based domestic policy should be complemented with asset-based policy because, while income-based policies ensure that consumption needs (including food, child care, rent, clothing, and health care) are met, asset-based policies provide the means to achieve greater independence and economic well-being.

It goes further to state the purposes of the program:

The purposes of this title are to provide for the establishment of demonstration projects designed to determine:

(1) the social, civic, psychological, and economic effects of providing to individuals and families with limited means an incentive to accumulate assets by saving a portion of their earned income;

(2) the extent to which an asset-based policy that promotes saving for postsecondary education, homeownership, and microenterprise development may be used to enable individuals and families with limited means to increase their economic self-sufficiency; and

(3) the extent to which an asset-based policy stabilizes and improves families and the community in which the families live.[19]

To date, more than fifteen homes have been purchased, scores of participants have returned to school, and several have started their own business. At the time of this book's publication, there

---

19 Assets for Independence Act 42 USC 604 (1998).

were twenty-three active participants in ECCO's Savings Match program.

As mentioned earlier, ECCO brought the first GED program to East Cooper by partnering with Charleston County Schools. Prior to this, a student would have to drive across town to participate. The growth in our Empowerment classes forced the program to move to Trident Tech Mount Pleasant, our local community college. This seemed like a natural move, to have the GED classes let students meet in an environment of higher learning.

Basic computer classes and advanced computer skill classes also provide opportunities for advancement. These courses help East Cooper residents acquire the skills necessary to be successful in today's workforce, while also serving to increase the strength of the ECCO's OOPI.

ECCO WORKS

Upon the transformation of ECCO's mission, it was obvious that the best way to help someone become financially independent was through permanent employment. Searches for job training and employment ministries to assist people in finding sustainable work began. I asked grantors and other agencies that provided poverty relief for referrals. One grantor told me about Manchester Bidwell in Pittsburgh, Pennsylvania. When I visited there, I saw that it offered on-the-job training for chefs, lab assistants, clerical workers, and even art professionals. It was overwhelming and very impressive: the organization's forty-thousand-square-foot greenhouse trained horticulturists, the campus restaurant taught cooking staff, chemistry labs equipped lab techs, the pottery studio allowed artists to learn to express their thoughts, and there was a sound studio where music artists and sound techs were trained. I realized it was more like a technical college than an employment connection.

Multiple folders and notebooks were made with information about workforce development programs around the country: from Delancey Street in San Francisco to Cascade Industries in Battle Creek, Michigan, I found models of employment for the unemployable. We also made personal visits to other local organizations within a few hours of driving. I knew I had to narrow my focus because ECCO already had so many programs to operate and maintain.

When I read *Why Don't They Just Get a Job*, by Dave Phillips, it caught my attention, so I began communicating with this author and founder of Cincinnati Works in Cincinnati, Ohio. Dave began the project almost twenty years ago and had an 85 percent success rate of helping the unemployed keep a job for one year. Phone calls and emails resulted in a visit to Cincinnati to see the success story firsthand; I was convinced a visit was necessary to learn what Dave was doing. Our director of empowerment and I wanted to see if their program was adaptable to our situation.

Two staff members and a board member joined me on a return trip, during which we saw a fluid organization that served the unemployed create lives that became self-sustainable. Even though Cincinnati was a world with a multitude of differences from ours—including 10 percent unemployment among a much-higher population—we thought we could emulate some of the program's essential elements back home.

While clients enrolled in the education and empowerment classes in Cincinnati also received healthy meals and snacks while participating in financial literacy training, goal setting, job preparedness, interview skills, resume writing, and the unspoken rules of the workplace, the significant component that set the program apart from all the other programs we studied and visited was the case manager or job coach. The job coach was assigned to the participant once she was employed and would then work with her for two years, acting as an intermediary between her and her new supervisor. Should there be a complaint about her performance as an employee, the job coach would meet with the participant and explain the position of the employer. The idea was to have her, as a worker, better understand the position of her employer, which many times was interpreted by the employee as being singled out for scrutiny.

Another important part of the Cincinnati Works program was its vow to undergird the employee for the same two-year period by offering other services, including financial assistance, counseling, housing, and child care. We saw that this approach would work well at ECCO with the broad array of services we offered. Basic and health services would provide ample avenues of support.

When we returned home, we held meetings and formed agreements with local employers, including Wild Dunes, the town of Mount Pleasant, Target, Cactus Car Wash, and others. The agreements arranged for graduates of our program to be interviewed. But after holding a couple of classes, we realized there weren't as many unemployed in East Cooper as in inner-city Cincinnati. So we adapted the model to fit our community. Goodwill Industries now has a Job Link Center in our building, which offers assistance in job searching and resume writing. ECCO still provides case management with our job coach and support for two years.

Outstanding staff and volunteers have allowed ECCO to develop these programs. Over the years, the programs have changed to become more relevant and efficient to help lead our clients to financial independence. The new mission and purpose of ECCO set in 2008 created a new direction to serve the needs of the poor and working poor more effectively and efficiently.

Putting a value on the classes held each year is next to impossible. Totaling the community impact compared to the costs is as follows:

PROGRAM IMPACT VALUES		
Program	Impact Values	ECCO Costs
Volunteers	$629,870	$40,000
Food	$750,000	$36,500
Clothing	$210,000	0
Dental	$1,100,000	$133,757
Prescription	$791,000	$69,991
Partners in Healthcare	$89,000	$30,000
Totals	$3,569,870	$310,248

Numbers tell the importance of a nonprofit against the government's retail cost of providing human and health services. Less than 10 percent of the costs reveal the efficiency of the contribution nonprofit organizations can provide the community. The effectiveness is demonstrated by the volunteers and staff who have a passion for the cause of the organization. ECCO provides low-cost services with a huge impact to the community and a monetary savings to local taxpayers.

Job Link Center grand opening: (L to R) Jack Little; town council member, Mark Smith; president and CEO of Palmetto Goodwill Industries, Bob Smith; and town council member, Thomasina Stokes Marshall.

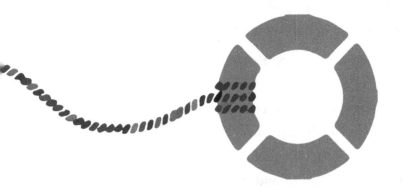

CHAPTER 11
Entering a
Community

Nobody likes strangers. As a huge Andy Griffith fan, I remember one episode of the popular show being about a stranger who came to town. The show's main characters were in the barbershop when a man got off the bus, walked to the barbershop, entered, and began greeting everyone by name. All the men were spooked: "How did he know our names?" they asked. When he left the barbershop, he greeted a lady by name who was passing by. The men all gathered and asked Andy, the town sheriff, what he was going to do about this stranger, to which he replied, "He ain't done nothing outside the law, so I ain't gonna do nothing." It turned out the stranger had been reading the Mayberry newspaper for years and decided he wanted to retire in the friendly community. But the stranger needed to take things slower because the residents tried to run him out of town when he attempted to fit in a little too fast. We are all suspicious by nature.

Getting involved in the community must be planned and deliberately carried through. The ministry of presence is essential when entering into a new community to begin a solid outreach ministry. After a while, residents begin to recognize visitors, and they begin talking with each other about those visitors. Many organizations will go in and distribute fliers and post information but never go into the community. Going into a community means building relationships.

Every community is different. They each have their own dynamics of leadership, hidden rules, management, acceptable and unacceptable behaviors and routines, and strengths and weaknesses. Communities can vary from week to week as a result of tenants residing in motels, mobile home parks, apartments, government-subsidized housing, and housing projects alongside homes where people have lived for generations. I have conducted community assessments in wealthy communities and skid row motels. After working in so many varying communities, the most important lesson I learned is that in order to learn and understand its unique characteristics, each community has to be dealt with individually.

An annual board retreat focused on Carter Lupton's book *Toxic Charity*. The objective of the retreat was to look at our mind-set (policy, attitude, and ministry) of providing our services at no cost to the recipient. Were we enabling rather than empowering? Were we creating people to be dependent or independent?

At the end of the first night's session, a board member and community leader uttered her first word of the retreat. She told everyone, "You don't know what you're talking about." Her comment caught everyone off guard. She said it again. "You're talking about what is in a book. You don't know what it's really like. You've never been in those communities." To her point: it's one thing to know where the community is, but until you get to know the people, there will never be a true relationship built.

The most effective way of entering a community is to conduct a community needs survey. Permission must be obtained from the management or communal leaders; these gatekeepers must be approached and treated with respect. The manager should not only be seen as the authority but also as a friend. A lot can be learned through listening to his insights and understanding the vision and hope for the community. The purpose of the survey must be shared up front, and the manager must always be kept informed and aware of any successes or failures.

A community needs assessment is done by receiving input from residents. The most common assessment is a door-to-door survey. Surveyors must introduce themselves and explain the purpose of the survey, but more often than not, they will still be met with suspicion. Trust must be earned, so it is important to remain friendly and cooperative. Questions can range from individual interests to needs and problems in the area. When the survey is completed and results compiled, an appointment with the manager is absolutely necessary to share the results with him personally. The residents also want to hear feedback, which can be accomplished individually or in an open forum.

THE NEEDS OF LOW-INCOME COMMUNITIES

Once, I initiated a ministry in an inner-city housing project and did the usual door-to-door survey asking about the interests and needs of the community. I was surprised with the responses. Most think people in the inner city want handouts like food or clothing. But this wasn't the case. The answers were safety, cleanliness, better community among the residents, and the enforcement of speed limits and activities for the neighborhood children.

I'm not trying to stereotype the needs and interests of the residents living in the inner city but rather trying to point out that when dealing with larger communities, plans must also meet immediate physical, health, material, spiritual, and economic needs.

Since ECCO serves a largely rural area, it's important to look at the needs of other comparable communities. Noted minister and civil rights activist John M. Perkins founded ministries in rural Mississippi that included a wide variety of programs: day care, farming coops, health centers, adult education centers, low-income housing developments, tutoring, job training, youth internships, and college scholarship programs, as well as very rigorous evangelism and church planting. Perkins came to the conclusion that government programs failed to address the deeper sources of hopelessness in low-income communities.

Assessments can also help to identify strengths of the individuals and community. When strengths are identified, they can be built upon. This allows lower-income communities to establish confidence and realize they can help themselves.

After doing the necessary homework of assessments, getting involved in the community allows residents to see that the interest has been sincere and that actions are being taken. Too many times, residents never see any action after surveys have been done; they have experienced numerous empty promises with no follow-up. After building their hopes and expectations, they are let down and become extremely disappointed.

But seeing new and continuous activity in a community begins to validate any efforts and promises made. Once one or two residents join in the activity, others will follow. Trust is then built and progress is made.

Mark Gornik, director of City Seminary of New York in Harlem, says, "Community development means the people and leaders of the community are the primary agents of action. The community residents themselves must be the main focus of analysis and planning," and they must be in control of the type and pace of change that will affect their families, lives, and economic life. Any other kind of help usually keeps residents in dependency because it doesn't bring social and economic capital into their neighborhood.

Another lesson to learn is that you must be invited in. Too many times, we assume that because we are offering good to a community, we will be readily welcomed in and accepted. This is the most overlooked mistake organizations make. No matter how much good you do, there is still an inherent mistrust of the people coming in.

Once, I heard a story about the dynamics of being a part of a community when you're an outsider coming in. Major metropolitan areas always have hospitals and medical centers that want to improve the health in low-income communities. Washington D.C. is no different. In this story, a local medical center invested hundreds of thousands of dollars in a mobile medical unit to help the underserved throughout the D.C. metropolitan area.

One Saturday, the costly unit entered its first inner-city housing project. The expectations of the medical center's staff were that residents would receive their outreach with excitement and spread the news about this godsend throughout the community. The unit pulled into the project and put out its signs and banners.

The first hour went by. No one came. The second hour passed. The doctors and nurses waited. No one showed. Lunch time came and went. Still no one. As this Saturday progressed, with all the money spent and time donated by the professionals, there was no response from the community.

The staff could not believe it. Not one resident came or even inquired about the free health services. The higher-ups of the medical center convened the next Monday and discussed the disappointment. Where did they go wrong? What could they do differently to help the underserved in this housing project?

The conclusion was reached, "No one knew." Of course no one would come if they didn't know it was there!

When the clinic came a month later for the second time, fliers were distributed and volunteers attached them to every door throughout the community. To add more excitement, the medical center hired a group of clowns to walk the sidewalks and extend the invitation about this great opportunity. They were playing fun soul music from the unit. Too much to ignore, right? No. It wasn't. Still, no one came.

At the end of the afternoon with not one single response, a worker went over to a resident, a black senior citizen, and after introducing herself asked, "Where is everyone? We have spent a lot of money, recruited volunteers, and put a bunch of time in our effort. Not one of your neighbors has responded or shown any interest. Can you tell me why?" she asked. The resident, jaded from years of unfulfilled promises reflecting an excess of do-gooding and traveling roadshows, said proudly, "No one invited you."

It's imperative the community must invite an organization into itself. The story drives home the point that an organization has to become accepted into the neighborhood for it to carry on long-term ministry.

So how do you become accepted to the point where the residents want you to become one of them? Too much too early can be damaging in establishing a new program. It takes time and patience. It takes faith knowing that opportunities will develop. You have to get to know the community; they must know both your face and your level of sincerity. It's one thing to know where the community is, but until you get to know the people, there will never be a true relationship. You have to earn their trust.

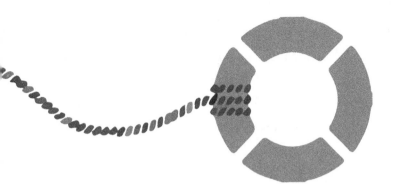

CHAPTER 12
Expanding Our Mission

P atience with goals and objectives has never been my strongest suit. Visions can be seen, and then I expect them to happen tomorrow. Just ask my staff. They would tell you I'm very impatient in my work, which differs from my personal life.

The previous chapter explained how it is necessary to involve the input and participation of the residents. This can be a time-consuming effort, but it is well worth the time investment. Projects need to lead by the community and its leaders.

In late 2013, an amazing thing happened. Several people approached me about beginning an ECCO location in the Cainhoy/Wando/Huger community. It seemed the stars had aligned.

Board member and Pastor Dr. Rev. Stephen Love in Huger told me the residents were interested in having an ECCO in their area. Around the same time and out of the blue, ECCO's founder, Monsignor James Carter of Christ our King Catholic Church, told me he was interested in opening a location in the Cainhoy/Huger area. His vision was to have a location that would house several agencies like Meals on Wheels and Habitat for Humanity. Not long after, Matt Sloan of the Daniel Island Company, a local developer of a high-end community, contacted me about that community's interest in supporting a program similar to ECCO. All this happened within a few months of each other. This is how I always see God at work—unexplainable things begin coming together.

To better understand the essence of these requests, you must have some background of the area and the people we serve. There are four points that need to be made. First, approximately 20 percent of our constituents come from this predominately black community. Second, this lower corner of Berkeley County is a stark contrast from the rest of the county. The community has a population of more than 4,500 residents. The area is isolated from the rest of the county and the county seat, which is twenty miles away from where public services are provided. Third, no human assistance services are located in the immediate community.

Fourth, transportation is a major obstacle for residents, as travel from Huger to Moncks Corner requires almost thirty minutes. ECCO is a twenty-mile journey in the opposite direction.

A planning session at the center with residents and ECCO staff.

In January 2014, several open forums with community leaders were held. We listened for two months. Discussions centered on the challenges facing the local families. Residents were included in a survey to determine the specific services they wanted. With this information, we formalized a comprehensive service plan for the satellite facility to incorporate the community's identified priorities such as medical and dental care, health education, home repair, education and job readiness, and after-school homework programs. East Cooper Meals on Wheels plans to use the site as a drop-off point for local volunteers to deliver them. East Cooper Habitat and Operation Home will have an office there as well. In light of the survey's conclusion, the community invited us to begin a local outreach in Huger.

The important point here is that the community invited us in. We did not want to just show up and say we are here to give you what we think you need. Local ownership was imperative to its success. This was the practice of my almost thirty years of starting churches and programs; having the church or community involved was the difference. This situation was no different—the residents needed to know this was theirs. Our goal was not to work for them; we wanted to work with them. This is empowerment—helping someone achieve what they could not do by themselves.

We all need empowering. My board advises and empowers me to be the best executive director I can be. When someone begins a new job or even a hobby, we are dependent on someone else's wisdom and knowledge. A coach empowers a player. When the athlete succeeds, the coach can bask in the knowledge that he was a part of that success. Everyone needs empowering.

It's important to point out that the Huger survey showed no interest in our emergency food, clothing, or financial assistance services. This indicated the residents were really interested in financial independence and living healthy lives.

Rev. Love discovered an empty 3,600-square-foot modular unit, which had served as a Head Start for several years. He negotiated a temporary lease with the owner so that it could be used by the community. The owner would allow it to be used if there was programming taking place, so Love started an after-school tutoring program for younger school-aged kids. In actuality, he secured it for the new ECCO satellite. He asked six churches to appoint two representatives to form a committee to oversee the building and its activities. The committee named it the Baldwin Carson Community Outreach Center (BCCOC). The name was derived from two families who had sold the two-acre property to Head Start.

On my first visit, I noticed the building's name was posted on the bulletin board. This affirmed our plan of the project being community owned. ECCO's role was to supply the services, and the community would provide volunteers. The BCCOC committee and I met many times to plan its future. Every step of the way, it was important for the committee to be involved and to approve of the plans being made.

We had to renovate the building for it to accommodate the services and programming desired by the residents. A computer lab was set up with fifteen computers. An office and a small computer lab were converted into medical examination rooms. The appliances in the commercial kitchen that had been removed were replaced, and we designed the space to be an instructional kitchen to teach healthy cooking. Cubicles were brought in to create office space for the staff. And of course, since it was a Head Start building, the small toilets had to be replaced with upgraded, adult-sized toilets!

Huger computer lab

The members of the BCCOC committee eagerly accepted all these changes, and they were eager to get things started. I also spoke with a woman in the gym where I work out, who told me how excited the community was about what we were doing. I am thankful I have had the opportunity to work with these wonderful folks. They are very compassionate and smart and have guided me in the best direction.

In only a few months, more than $370,000 was raised to renovate the facility and provide services for three years. The funding partners committed to be involved in the program were Christ Our King Catholic Church, Daniel Island Community Fund, Benefitfocus, Roper Healthcare, Nucor Steel, and BP.

Speaking of my impatience, I could have done it all in two or three months, or so I think. But as I've said, taking time and developing relationships along the way is crucial. ECCO began classes and services at the BCCOC in July 2015. It took one and a half years of laying groundwork in the community, but that is not uncommon.

It has been an amazing adventure. In three ministry positions, each organization I served has experienced significant growth, increased and generated revenue to support them, and recruited volunteers to carry them out. In making the decision to go into the ministry, I accepted to trust that the Lord would provide. My story is due to Him and His faithfulness.

WANT TO KNOW MORE ABOUT ECCO?

There are several ways to learn more about ECCO and get involved:

Visit www.ECCOcharleston.org and subscribe to our newsletter, read blog posts, or make a donation online.

Follow ECCO on social media—you can easily engage with a quick like, share, or comment.

Our greatest need is always for financial support.
Donations can be mailed to:
ECCO Development Office
1145 Six Mile Road
Mount Pleasant, SC 29466

We would love to give you our "Tour of Hope"—call us at (843) 849-9220 if you are in the area.

Printed in the USA
CPSIA information can be obtained
at www.ICGtesting.com
JSHW012052140824
68134JS00035B/3387

9 781599 326265